THE SUSTAINABLE NATION: POLITICS, ECONOMY AND JUSTICE

ADVANCES IN SUSTAINABILITY AND ENVIRONMENTAL JUSTICE

Previously ADVANCES IN ECOPOLITICS
Series Editor: Liam Leonard

PUBLISHED UNDER SERIES TITLE **'ADVANCES IN SUSTAINABILITY AND ENVIRONMENTAL JUSTICE'**

International Business, Sustainability and Corporate Social Responsibility Volume 11
Edited by Maria Alejandra Gonzalez-Perez and Liam Leonard

Principles and Strategies to Balance Ethical, Social and Environmental Concerns with Corporate Requirements Volume 12
Edited by Maria Alejandra Gonzalez-Perez and Liam Leonard

Environmental Philosophy: The Art of Life in a World of Limits Volume 13
Edited by Liam Leonard, John Barry, Marius De Geus, Peter Doran and Graham Parkes

The Sustainability of Restorative Justice Volume 14
Edited by Paula Kenny and Liam Leonard

Occupy the Earth: Global Environmental Movements Volume 15
Edited by Liam Leonard and Sya Buryn Kedzior

The UN Global Compact: Fair Competition and Environmental and Labour Justice in International Markets Volume 16
Edited by Maria Alejandra Gonzalez-Perez and Liam Leonard

Beyond the UN Global Compact: Institutions and Regulations Volume 17
Edited by Liam Leonard and Maria Alejandra Gonzalez-Perez

Lessons from the Great Recession: At the Crossroads of Sustainability and Recovery Volume 18
Edited by Constantin Gurdgiev, Liam Leonard and Maria Alejandra Gonzalez-Perez

Climate Change and the 2030 Corporate Agenda for Sustainable Development Volume 19
Edited by Liam Leonard

Environmental Criminology: Spatial Analysis and Regional Issues Volume 20
Edited by Liam Leonard

ADVANCES IN SUSTAINABILITY AND ENVIRONMENTAL JUSTICE VOLUME 21

THE SUSTAINABLE NATION: POLITICS, ECONOMY AND JUSTICE

BY

LIAM LEONARD
California State University, Los Angeles, CA, USA

emerald PUBLISHING

United Kingdom – North America – Japan
India – Malaysia – China

Emerald Publishing Limited
Howard House, Wagon Lane, Bingley BD16 1WA, UK

First edition 2018

British Library Cataloguing in Publication Data
A catalogue record for this book is available from the British Library

ISBN: 978-1-78743-380-9 (Print)
ISBN: 978-1-78743-379-3 (Online)
ISBN: 978-1-78743-459-2 (Epub)

ISSN: 2051-5030 (Series)

Printed and bound by CPI Group (UK) Ltd, Croydon, CR0 4YY

ISOQAR
REGISTERED
Certificate Number 1985
ISO 14001

ISOQAR certified Management System, awarded to Emerald for adherence to Environmental standard ISO 14001:2004.

INVESTOR IN PEOPLE

CONTENTS

ACKNOWLEDGMENTS

The author would like to thank all of the staff at Emerald Publishing for their assistance with this and all the volumes in the *Ecopolitics and Sustainable Justice* series. In addition, he wishes to thank all contributors, editors and reviewers who have made the series a success over the last decade. Finally, he wishes to thank his family for their support, and in particular Janice Harter for her encouragement.

CHAPTER 1

INTRODUCTION: THE IRISH STATE, FROM BOOM TO BAILOUT TO BREXIT

This volume of the *Advances in Sustainability and Environmental Justice* examines events which occurred in the Republic of Ireland in the early decades of the Millennium. These years have proved to be tumultuous for Ireland, with major events such as the Peace Process, the economic boom and subsequent collapse of the Irish economy, the bailout plan of the International Monetary Fund (IMF). More recently, the United Kingdom's decision to leave the European Union has their Irish neighbours with an island divided North and South by an EU border. Plans in June 2017 for a coalition between the Conservatives and the Democratic Unionist Party of Northern Ireland, which goes against the spirit of the Good Friday Agreement, add to a disruptive air of uncertainty in the Republic. The main focus of this book is the response to policy processes which have occurred within the context of these dramatic changes.

Essentially, the book can be divided into three main sections, Politics, Economy and Justice. The book will provide an examination and analysis of the infrastructural development and social justice strategies and subsequent community responses in the Republic of Ireland, over recent decades. We can understand the subtext of development policies in Ireland in the context of the nation's transition from a rights-based service policy model into a rationalised entity which reflects the prevailing outlook of neo-liberal governments globally. The impact of this neo-liberal/neo-corporatist policy framework has been outlined by Phelan and Norris (2008), where they write of the linkages between the prevailing policy model and the impact on poorer communities in Dublin. The community responses which emerge in reaction to the exclusion and concern caused by a corrosive form of 'social partnership' can also be understood in this light, as environmental disputes about energy policies and communities, transport policy and heritage, waste management policy and pollution, and development and water supplies reflect an ongoing concern with the impact of reckless development on communities, environments and the political process.

After decades of economic stagnation, the Irish state embraced the dualistic agendas of neo-liberalism and neo-corporatism to create the economic basis for the multinational-led development that came to be synonymous with the boom decade of the 'Celtic Tiger'. In addition, the state prioritised unfettered (or unregulated) infrastructural development as a response to the social needs of communities traditionally marginalised by high levels of unemployment and emigration. We can understand the consequences of this shift from the provision of a service-based social policy platform into that of a policy framework which promotes industrial concerns in the context of the Irish state's prevailing neo-liberal model, which has resulted in a social partnership model where the industrial lobby holds sway, dominating successive populist governments with the support of compliant trade unions.

One result of this has seen areas traditionally marginalised due to the deprivation of poverty, unemployment and emigration, embarking on collective action responses in defence of communities or environments (Leonard, 2008). In many ways, it has been the manner in which rural communities have been neglected by the state over the decades before the Celtic Tiger which has created the pool of discontent from which campaigns of opposition to state policy have emerged. The resultant tension between environmental and developmental considerations has created a conflict where 'the state should mediate to promote the common good' (Allen, 2007, p. xvii). However, in the Irish case, the demands of industry have gained prevalence over those of local communities excluded from neo-corporatist arrangements, with a series of community-based environmental protests occurring as a result in recent years.

These disputes have occurred against a backdrop of rapid economic growth, with communities now experiencing a change of lifestyle, with an increasingly flexible workforce now reliant on commuting to and from industrial centres, as housing has come to be priced out of the budgets of many in the population, including those migrants who have come to Ireland in search of employment. Even the protection of the trade unions has come to be diminished, owing to neo-corporate demands on social policy:

> In Ireland, pressure for flexibility and work intensity comes directly through social partnership agreements. Whereas in the past workers were granted pay rises in response to rising rates of inflation, today they must first show 'verifiable' improvements in productivity to get a pay rise ... outside of the world of work the corporations want to hollow out what is left of social rights or the social wage. (Allen, 2007, p. 11)

Such demands have placed a strain on the traditional 'social capital' which had been the bedrock of community life in rural Ireland, as families become caught up in a cycle of overtime, commuting and crèches. At the same time, the remaining vestiges of a welfare state have been all but replaced with a regime of a privatised health industry. The mistreatment of immigrants in the workforce has led to unions becoming concerned about a 'race to the bottom' in relation to the work and welfare practice of the neo-liberal state (Allen, 2007, pp. 36–37). Ultimately, there is increased uncertainty as to whether prosperity has come at too high of a price:

> The urgent question concerns the relationship between economic and cultural modernisation: is being happier the realisation of the good life? Does the Celtic Tiger represent an improvement in our overall quality of life, or moral bankruptcy and spiritual dereliction? (Kuhling & Keohane, 2007, p. 4)

This transition from policies aimed at providing services to those embedded in industrial practice is reflected in the Irish environmental policy agendas. These policy frameworks had originally been devised in order to prevent pollution and regulate industry, but have subsequently come to facilitate corporations and economic growth.

Having enjoyed the benefits of the economic growth associated with the Celtic Tiger boom of the last decade, communities in Ireland are beginning to witness the downside of accelerated growth. Offshoots of rapid development such as hyper-consumption, a buoyant property market and increased car ownership led to further demand for critical infrastructure such as roads, waste management sites and water treatment facilities. Such was the link between growth and infrastructure that those communities which voiced concerns about projects were deemed to be backward thinking and against progress. An understanding of these issues can be derived from an examination of the community responses to infrastructural projects that came to be perceived as threats to locals and their health and environment, or to the heritage of the nation itself.

Prior to this, political groupings had supported a number of environmental community movements which had mobilised against infrastructural projects in rural and suburban areas. The book examines some of these contentious disputes, including issues surrounding the municipal provision of water and attempts to develop a gas installation and pipeline in the west of Ireland. Such movements became characteristic in an Ireland that was experiencing accelerated growth in the early decades of this century. While many welcomed growth, some warned of an economy which was overheating and which excluded many, including the poor, women's groups and community groups concerned for their local environments (Leonard, 2008).

This increase in marginalisation is examined in the book's final chapters, as issues of justice and injustice are discussed. These chapters look at Ireland's increased multiculturalism, and the need to develop new perspectives to create an inclusive Ireland. In addition, approaches to restorative justice and imprisonment are examined, as part of attempts to create what this author has titled 'Sustainable Justice' (Leonard & Kenny, 2010).

This book represents a culmination of my research on Ireland which began at the turn of the Millennium. Whilst some of the issues here have been published in part in journals, books and articles through different formats, this book has given me an opportunity to revisit, revise and distil my work on Ireland from the last two decades. These have indeed been tumultuous changes in Ireland over these years, from the Peace Process through to the 100th anniversary of the Easter Rising in 2016. One wonders what rebel leaders such as Padraig Pearse, James Connolly, Constance Markievicz and Michael Collins would think of the current political establishment in Ireland, which has succumbed to austerity and neo-liberal corporatism rather than embracing their communities and resources in a sustainable manner.

And as the *Advances in Sustainability and Environmental Justice* comes of age with this, its 21st volume, I have been pleased to see the series grow through the years examined in this book. I am certain that the series will continue to grow and explore relevant issues in sustainability for many years to come.

REFERENCES

Allen, K. (2007). *The corporate takeover of Ireland*. Dublin: Irish Academic Press Ltd.

Kuhling, C., & Keohane, C. (2007). *Cosmopolitan Ireland: Globalisation and quality of life*. London: Pluto Press.

Leonard, L. (2008). *The environmental movement in Ireland*. Dordrecht: Springer.

Leonard, L., & Kenny, P. (2010). Sustainable justice & the community advances in ecopolitics. *Advances in ecopolitics* (Vol. 6). Bingley/Bradford: Emerald.

Phelan, E., & Norris, M. (2008). Neo-corporatist governance of homeless services in Dublin: Reconceptualization, incorporation and exclusion. *Critical Social Policy*, *28*(1), 51–73.

CHAPTER 2

ECONOMY AND RESISTANCE☆

ABSTRACT

Ireland has witnessed a succession of community-based protests in recent years. Issues have included water charges, refuse collection taxes, infrastructural developments, incinerators, dumps and toxic industries. This chapter will argue that the basis for these disputes is the Irish state's neo-liberal and neo-corporatist policy framework, which favours accelerated and reckless infrastructural development while excluding community concerns about health and environmental issues. The chapter will also examine the use of communications technologies, which form a large part of the modern economy, as a tool for community resistance.

Keywords: Community activism; exclusion; infrastructural development; communications technologies; media; social partnership

INTRODUCTION

Late 2016 witnessed the takeover of Apollo House, a large building in the centre of Dublin City, in protest of the city's increase in homelessness and poverty. Apollo House was held by the National Assets Management Agency (NAMA) on behalf of the Irish state, and represented the fallacy of Ireland's ruling elite which had presided over. Those involved in the takeover were musicians, artists, writers, activists and radicals, mirroring the backgrounds of the leaders of the 1916 Rising against British Rule, which the Irish government had spent millions on while enforcing austerity measures on behalf of the International Monetary Fund (IMF). The path to austerity and the Irish state's bailout of its financial sector followed on from successive scandals involving major Irish institutions such as the political, religious, banking and business sectors.

☆Some of this article was originally published in Leonard (2009).

Ireland had soon succumbed to the politics of privilege once the uprising against British rule and subsequent Civil War had ended in 1922. The new political elites in the Irish Free State and their successors after the Republic of Ireland came into being in 1949 were characterised by a deep conservatism, and austere politics, social repression and massive waves of emigration were the norm in Ireland. Even the phase of economic growth experienced in the short-lived "Celtic Tiger" years between 1996 and 2004 were built on a house of sand, as corruption between the political and industrial sector led to an economic collapse, leading to the departure of a new wave of young Irish emigrants to destinations across the globe.

As Irish development theorist Peader Kirby (2006, p. 182) has put it:

> For all the illusion of success, Ireland flies on one wing as long as it allows (indeed, actually actively fosters through public policy) the enrichment of an elite and the marginalisation of growing numbers of its citizens from the benefits of economic growth.

The accelerated and reckless nature of Irish development which emerged from this tryst has resulted in a series of protests by communities concerned about environmental and health risks posed by this policy direction which has arisen under the auspices of neo-liberal 'social partnership', but represents in reality the triumph of neo-liberalism, naked greed and which led to poor planning and lax regulatory practices.

Essentially, we can understand the subtext of social policy in Ireland in the context of a transition of social and environmental policy from a rights-based service into a rationalised entity which reflects the prevailing outlook of Ireland's neo-liberal government and its neo-corporatist 'partnership' model. The impact of this neo-liberal/neo-corporatist policy framework has been highlighted by Phelan and Norris (2008), where they write of the linkages between the prevailing policy model and the impact on individual services such as services for the homeless in Dublin. The community responses which emerge in reaction to the exclusion and concern caused by a corrosive form of 'social partnership' can also be understood in this light, as environmental disputes about resource policy and communities, transport policy and heritage, waste management policy and pollution, and development and water supplies reflect an ongoing concern with the impact of reckless development on communities, environments and the political process.

As the following section will show, the Irish public's ability to mobilise around communications technologies became a significant part of community group resistance to austerity.

THE ECONOMY, MEDIA AND RESISTANCE

A notable feature of the post-bailout political landscape in Ireland has been the increasing incidents of confrontation between communities and elites. These conflicts have occurred in the wake of the declining relevance of the traditional left-right dichotomy, and have been exemplified by the campaigns of opposition led by community groups against the state and corporate sectors. One notable area of economic activity which has also been utilised by community movements is the use of communications technologies. The use of text, internet and media technologies by protest groups has facilitated the growth of a network of committed activists, who provide scientific and technological expertise to like-minded protests around the globe. By exploring campaign's use of media and internet technologies, we can understand the significance of new approaches taken by grassroots groups as part of their resistance to state, corporate and institutional actors. The community's ability to utilise communications technologies to forge links with local and global anti-movements provides evidence of the extensive nature of the links available to grassroots groups.

Communication technologies enhance protest movements by providing leverage and influence for grassroots groups in an era characterised by knowledge flows and technocratic expertise. Internet linkages facilitate innovative approaches to political opportunity structures for movements through emergent features of protest that create a new nexus of capabilities in the globalised era. These cycles of protest of new social movements have come to be underpinned by the onset of interactive knowledge flows, networked alliances, improved tactical approaches and advanced mobilisational capabilities through the development of diverse protest strategies.

The use of internet technology as a basis for support between disparate protest groups is strategically augmented by the utilisation of media networks eager for a steady supply of presentable items on potential ecological crises for their ceaseless broadcasts. The web has become a vehicle for the dissemination of the various components of the environmental movement: academic and scientific expertise, political strategies, legal frameworks and the location of globalised support networks. By facilitating the spread of information which enhances campaigns of protest, the new technologies of communication have become a vital tool in the arsenal of various Irish protest groups advocating for the homeless or for water rights and other areas of social and environmental justice.

Castells defines internet technologies as a 'privileged tool for acting, informing, recruiting, organising and counter-dominating' (2001, p. 137). Through the application of communication technologies, localised environmental movements can link with similar groups on a global basis, learning from the hard earned experiences of previous campaigns. This has transformed the once-isolated pockets of environmental resistance into a world-wide movement able to challenge transnational corporate polluters, in the place of regional campaigns of resistance. The increasing reliance on communication technologies by environmental groups has seen a transformation in activists' profiles; changing from the politically dogmatic campaigner to that of a media-friendly professional with a high level of expertise in a related field. This use of expertise has created what Castells has called 'the new dynamics of social movements' (2001, p. 138).

While internet sabotage from computer 'hackers' is an established strategy of the politics of the information age, it is the ability of social movements to mobilise and communicate through information technologies which provides a degree of dynamic innovation to the politics of protest. The internet has become the activists' meeting house in the information era. Networks of opposition have been established and continue to reinforce protests globally, with such success that industries and institutions are now attempting to restructure their own practices in response to the new cultural and political expression of environmental values. This process of redefining cultural values has traditionally been part of old social movement agendas, however, internet technologies make this redefinition or reinterpretation of values much easier for relevant movements today.

This shift in social movement capabilities can be seen in the transition of protest groups from a reactive force for change within a dominant ideological paradigm to that of a cultural movement which can set the campaign agendas as seen in the political campaigns of progressives such as Bernie Saunders in the United States. In turn, old political conflicts can have their overall boundaries redrawn in this era of communication technologies, as cultural values are redefined through information flows. In this way, old political values (and conflicts) can be resurrected through a campaign based on communication of new perspectives.

The restructuring of political and cultural values through the technologies of communication has become an important strategy for social movements in their campaigns of action. It is what Castells refers to as 'mobilisation around meaning' (2001, p. 140). The importance of new political understandings of meanings becomes evident in relation to the crisis of legitimation facing democratic politics. As mainstream politics veers towards a centrist, liberal democratic monolith, radical political expression has adopted new organisational forms, with traditional hierarchies replaced by internet links which can give equal voice to a multitude of concerned activists, each able to give as much or as little to a campaign as internet technology allows.

Furthermore, social movements' campaigns are now structured around the technologies of communication. The medium can affect the message, and often shape it. For instance, a movement's success or failure may be based on media depictions of certain aspects of a campaign, rather than being perceived on any subsequent outcome. Public attitudes are swayed by media images of homeless or water charges protestors in media news reports. Campaigns gain a large amount of public support for their movement from the transmission of these images. Ultimately, the media is utilised to create transferable emotiveness around a political event, through the creation of a moral frame.

The link between internet mobilisation of protests and satellite news coverage became evident from the events surrounding the 'Occupy' and anti-globalisation protests in the United States. These protests and the massive publicity they received from global media networks has elevated protest to a new level, giving symbolic meanings and outlets for political expression to a new generation of activists. Issues of significance for young people, such as anti-corporatism or environmentalism, can now be forced on to the agendas of powerful groups such as the IMF, with an immediacy that by-passes the slow and cumbersome cycle of parliamentary elections. The immediacy of internet communications increases the spontaneous nature of protest events, making them at once attractive to both the casual activist and the media networks which follow these events.

The emergence of global networks of disaffected young people has enhanced many Irish community movement's ability to mobilise campaigns against austerity. Throughout the last decade a new generation of politically motivated activists with advanced networking capabilities has become part of the discourse of new millennium politics, as characterised by the success in campaigns who have seen nuclear power, fracking and genetically modified organisms (GMOs) outlawed in the Republic of Ireland. Communication technologies are a central component of consumer activism that targets sweatshop production by Nike or unsustainable modes of transport such as sports utility vehicles (SUVs). Cyber protesters can challenge economic multinationals that are now recognised as 'the most powerful political forces of our time' (Klein, 1999).

For protest movements, the internet allows for a strategic diversity which prevents such movements from becoming stifled by drawn-out campaigns which can sap morale. Through communication technologies, the battleground for protests can be shifted at the press of a keyboard button. This immediacy gives protest movements the ability to link and mobilise with key allies globally. Key events are utilised as mobilisation strategies, resulting in the expansion of democratic deficit and moral frames through the filter of any ensuing media coverage. An example of this can be seen in the events around various protests in modern Ireland. As the police response to protest can be severe, the media coverage and public outcry about police actions on the day may lead to a prolongment of the event's salience with the media.

The ability to challenge globalised networks or power by protest movements has become an important aspect of the politics of the new century. As traditional institutions are increasingly redundant, new equations of power set grassroots protest movements against the globalised industrial–military complex. Communication technologies, once the preserve of the latter, have become the weapon of choice for the former. Strategically, the mobilisation, coordination and publicity needed for protest movements at a global level can only be achieved through communication networks. What becomes clear from an analysis of how protest movements utilise communication technologies is the increasing importance of these new forms of technology as a tool for spreading information and organising resistance. The new technologies of communication ultimately create a platform for forms of political resistance which can respond to the needs of concerned citizens in an increasingly globalised world.

Essentially, the strategic impact new media forms have had on protest movements has been based on a movement's ability to influence overall media agendas. The ratings potential of protest coverage is dependent on two main themes: the message of the movement, and the potential for an attention-grabbing media event emanating from that movement's activities.

Therefore, the subject of movement salience becomes a critical aspect of how media attention is maintained. According to Rogers and Dearing (1988), there are three main features in the issue maximisation process. These are part of an agenda building structure which incorporates factors such as feeding the insatiable appetites of communications elites such as multimedia corporations through the provision of movement events which embrace the spectacular, and a coordination of media, public and policy agendas. This fusion of demand, expectation and need shapes wider understandings of the contentious social events which will maintain public attention, as well as viewer ratings.

A central feature of this analysis is the importance of the issue in the context of social expectations. Issue salience is achieved through extensive media coverage, but the issues can only be ignited into activism through the intervention of movement entrepreneurs or gatekeepers. Issue importance is maintained by 'public' and 'policy agenda setting' (Dearing & Rogers, 1996). From this perspective, policy response to an issue is dependent on the importance such an issue is granted by public and media agendas. In this way, successful outcomes to social movement activity are demonstrated to be increasingly reliant on that movement's ability to influence professional media elites, in addition to provoking a public response to their issue of concern. Subsequently, the media's role in a new political equation, as a filter for conflicts between grassroots and elites, becomes a crucial aspect of the new political dynamic.

A further understanding of the centrality of media to the grassroots movements can be achieved through an analysis of what has been termed the 'editorial gatekeeper'. It is the role of such gatekeepers to decide what events in society are noteworthy enough to feature on front page or primetime news reports. Their importance to a grassroots movement in need of public support is paramount, far exceeding policy makers or other members of the bureaucratic elite. While political disputes still require the exchange of views from adversarial groups, the influence of media on the public perception of that dispute ultimately influences the outcome of political contestations.

What becomes evident from this analysis is the importance of media advocacy and editorial support for grassroots movements to gain leverage. In response to this challenge, movements have achieved a greater degree of media professionalism, combined with technological expertise. As the influence of advertisers increases, media coverage and subsequent editorial support can be effectively driven or censored by commercial demand. Another form of external pressure applied to media has been demonstrated by the US government's determined steering of the military action taken in Iraq and Afghanistan. In a new departure for war coverage, journalists were embedded with various regiments across the field of operations. Open criticism of the war led to public accusations of unpatriotic behaviour, and even treachery.

Invariably, the media's coverage of social events can be shaped by an underlying ideological perspective. The meanings of societal disputes around topics such as environmental or human rights are subject to an ideologically based conflict of definition. Here again, the media play a central role, ordaining the public perception of social issues, which is flavoured by inherent ideological demands. One result of this shift in social perception has seen an increased cultural significance of the aesthetics of political disputes. A further demonstration of the cultural significance of political media coverage can be gleaned from a study of the anti-globalisation phenomenon. This movement has drawn the lines of demarcation clearly, between a grassroots coalition and the formal institutions of global power, such as the IMF. In this way, the anti-globalisation movement allows potential activists the widest definition to associate themselves with certain sentiments with which many people feel some form of empathy. As a result, media coverage is guaranteed as a mass-mobilisation of a broad range of groups from academics to anarchists provides the potential for a 'media event', the focus of which is readily provided by the often heavy-handed response of local police and security agencies.

CONCLUSION

The shift in policy direction undertaken by successive neo-liberal Irish governments has led to increased conflict between communities and the state in relation to infrastructural projects and development. This new dispensation is best summed up by the following quote:

> The globalised, neo-liberal configuration is a profoundly decivilising moment .... In this context, the contemporary fetish for the accumulation of private wealth that has fuelled and over inflated the housing boom in Ireland is not a symbol of progress, but rather, is regressive, and represents the ascendance of the negative, barbaric side of the Enlightenment articulated by Adorno and Horkheimer .... (Kuhling & Keohane, 2007, p. 166)

While the Irish state has attempted to follow a neo-liberal policy framework set out by successive coalitions and backed by the social partners, the emphasis is firmly focused on economic growth over any other environmental protection or concerns for communities. Ultimately, the cost of this form of unregulated economic growth has led to greater environmental degradation and an undermining of significant aspects of the nation's heritage. In particular, rural communities have borne the cost of Ireland's transition from a rural agrarian society into an industrialised and globalised economy, and this has not been without its problems:

> So, while much of the transition has been positive, it has been accompanied by a widening gap between rich and poor; rising crime rates; increased environmental pollution; a large infrastructure deficit; a housing market that excludes many; a huge growth in long-distance

> commuting; health and welfare systems creaking under pressure; a weakening rural economy .... (Kitchin & Bartley, 2007, p. 304)

In conclusion, as communities across Ireland have paid the price over the state's policy of prioritising a neo-liberal form of development in order to underpin private wealth gathering and multinational investment, the policy models which emphasise inflated development and lax regulation may prove to be ill advised as fluctuations on local and global property markets continue. Peadar Kirby has written that 'the challenge of social inclusion, therefore takes us to the heart of the Irish growth model' (2006, p. 183). As Ireland's community's resistance to austerity continues, a new form of politics has emerged which seeks to place 'people before profit' and may yet give rise to a Republic worthy of its people.

REFERENCES

Castells, M. (2001). *The internet galaxy: Reflections on the internet*. Oxford: Oxford University Press.

Dearing, J., & Rogers, E. (1996). *Agenda-setting*. London: Sage.

Kirby, P. (2006). Bringing social inclusion to centre stage: Towards a project of active citizenship. In D. Jacobsen, P. Kirby, & D. Ó. Broin (Eds.), *Taming the tiger: Social exclusion in a globalised Ireland* (pp. 180–199). Dublin: New Island.

Kitchin, R., & Bartley, B. (2007). Conclusion: Ireland now and in the future. In B. Bartley & R. Kitchin (Eds.), *Understanding contemporary Ireland* (pp. 301–308). London: Pluto Press.

Klein, N. (1999). *No logo: Taking ain at brand bullies*. New York, NY: Random House.

Kuhling, C., & Keohane, C. (2007). *Cosmopolitan Ireland: Globalisation and quality of life*. London: Pluto Press.

Leonard, L. (2008). *The environmental movement in Ireland*. Dordrecht: Springer.

Leonard, L. (2009). Social partnership's boiling point: Environmental issues and social responses to neo-liberal policy in Ireland. *Critical Social Policy*, *29*(2), doi:10.1177/0261018308101630

Phelan, E., & Norris, M. (2008). Neo-corporatist governance of homeless services in Dublin: Reconceptualization, incorporation and exclusion. *Critical Social Policy*, *28*(1), 51–73.

Rogers, E. M., & Dearing, J. W. (1988). Agenda-setting research: Where has it been? Where is it going? In J. A. Anderson (Ed.), *Communication yearbook* (Vol. 11, pp. 555–594). Newbury Park, CA: Sage.

CHAPTER 3

CONSERVATION

ABSTRACT

This chapter will present an analysis of mobilisation, framing processes and outcomes of environmental conservation campaigns in Ireland. By locating contemporary disputes about the public space in Ireland within an understanding of this transition from a traditional rural and agrarian society into that of a modern industrialised and urbanised European state, a wider understanding of the circumstances surrounding such contests emerges.[1] *This form of analysis goes beyond a social narrative, and facilitates a fuller understanding of the consequences emanating from the framing and reframing of heritage within a context of a society where an obsession with history has been displaced by a zealous predilection for economic development.*

Keywords: Conservation; heritage; agrarian; rural; public space; framing

INTRODUCTION

While this transition from traditionalist concern to modernist utility has placed great strain on the environment and heritage of the nation, it has also created opportunities for widespread political mobilisation in successive decades during periods of economics growth or decline (Leonard, 2006, 2008). These outbreaks of collective action have provoked widespread debate and coverage in the media as several thousand people have taken part in heritage-based protests in Ireland over this period.

Nonetheless, a significant section of the Irish public have mobilised in response to threats to public spaces during a phase where people were characterised as being solely obsessed with financial gain and property. These sporadic outbreaks of collective action are a reminder that in Ireland as in most cultures, there are deeper concerns with space and place that go beyond material concerns or economics. Migrant and immigrant groups share this concern for spatially derived representation, rendering heritage as a most contested and culturally charged element of social construction. An instinctive or reflexive response to threats to public spaces has emerged during this series of heritage or community disputes. Such movements represent the articulation of indigenous monologues of communities who are embedded in the streets or landscapes of their towns and regions. Their rootedness may not always require a contemporary presence at the point of concern as the indigenous consciousness formed in the community inculcates an inherent compulsion to protect spaces rendered sacred through memory, loss and shared expression. When such localities are threatened, a mutuality of concern for collective folk memories and meanings in the guise of a shared heritage emerges as a significant grievance in the mobilisation of common cause. One consequence has been the emergence of an ongoing debate, alongside episodes of collective action around the ethical and moral considerations surrounding issues of heritage and conservation in a rapidly developing Ireland.

In attempting to understand heritage, many competing elements of nature and humanity may be evoked in an attempt to capture its underlying meanings. As with other cultures, Irish heritage contains a host of meanings and contexts carried through the portal of time as an inherent folk memory is rooted in the land or streetscape. While it is often stated that Ireland has a rich natural and built heritage, it can be difficult to find consensus on where this may be found, or what this heritage actually represents. What seems to be important is a sense of place and time embodying the natural beauty of God's creation or human endeavour, whether these are represented by buildings, battlefields or bogs. Writing in 1996, David Brett presents an interrogation of the 'concept of heritage' whereby meanalities, locations and processes have come to be understood through history. Throughout the evolutionary patterns of societal engagement with our natural and built hinterlands, we have come to represent and define ourselves as an autonomous group by way of undertaking a reinvention of the norms and ways which have emerged throughout the course of Irish history. One result of this new economic direction was an increased antipathy towards our natural and built environment as polluting industries and multinational or state infrastructure began to impinge on communities, landscapes and antiquities throughout the nation (Leonard, 2006). Furthermore, Hilary Tovey (1992, p. 275) has indicated that there has never been a period where a significant prioritisation of institutional conservation at any phase of Ireland's post-independence self-rule. It was as if the new state wished to erase the memory of the past by eradicating the cracked fanlights and facades of the nation's built environment while paving over its natural beauty and historical sites.

This dichotomy between the nationalist Irish state and those who were concerned with conservation can be traced back to the Unionist or pro-British leanings of early conservationists in Ireland. This group was concerned with maintaining the unionist heritage of the Anglo-Irish ascendancy class, along with their large estates. Many in the local Irish population had been uprooted to make way for these large demesnes, and a sense of resentment against this form of heritage and conservation simmered long after Ireland gained nominal independence from Britain in the 1920s. This set the Irish conservation movement back, as anti-conservation activities such as game poaching were seen as valid expressions of rebellion against the unionist authorities. This residue of hostility remains apparent in the populist rural opposition to *An Taisce*, the Irish Heritage Trust, which was viewed as a largely urban and anti-rural organisation by many local politicians and the popular press. While *An Taisce* has worked hard to address this residue, issues such as the location of houses in rural areas have tended to see battle lines redrawn along the traditional urban/conservationists versus rural populist divide.

As Tovey, Share, and Corcoran (2007) has noted, heritage groups such as the Irish Georgian Society took on the mantle of the 'moral entrepreneurs' (*ibid.*) of Dublin's built environment when the destruction of sections of the southern section of the city began in the 1970s. Faced with a hegemonic concern for development combined with attempts to wipe out unwanted aspects of the past, conservationists became the curators of a living history which was under threat from political elites and developers alike. Thomas Farel Heffernan[2] sets the inception of this curator's vigil around the time of excavation of the east-end of the cross block in Dublin Castle in 1961. In the era of John F Kennedy's presidency, Ireland's architectural heritage had been revealed in 'an exciting glimpse' (*ibid.*). Dublin's origins could be traced back to their ancient Viking and Norman past, with visible links to Celtic neighbours also evident (*ibid.*). This discovery provided visible confirmation that the remains of Viking Dublin contained a site which could represent the past. For Duncan and Ley (1993, p. 39), 'sites of representation' present a dualistic signification of place. However in postcolonial Ireland, this representation was contentious, as the disputes about Woodquay and Georgian Dublin would later prove. In many ways the heritage of the past in Ireland became a version of Edward Saids' understanding of an oppositional form of *the Other*[3] in an Ireland gripped by a modernist and postcolonial zeal for state led building. In such cases 'the Other' can be reclaimed from past representations by providing a 'familiar and useful' (Duncan & Ley, 1993, p. 39) utilisation for a contested site.

These sites of contested heritage provide us with what is essentially a 'cultural production' (Duncan, 1999, p. 54) which has come to be perceived in a variety of contexts throughout history. Moreover, this cultural production is at once linked to both structure and agency as society comes to comprehend culture and heritage through its potential uses rather than through any inherent value. Local authorities have been described as having certain methodologies which hamper any further valuation of heritage as all sites are invariably reduced to a set of uses such as 'production or consumption related activity ... private property or public service etc.' (Pickvance & Harloe, 1990; Saunders, 1986). What follows is a utilitarian hegemonic order which re-classifies heritage within the cultural assumptions of temporary elites. This hegemony can only be challenged through the presentation and cultural project of conservationist movements.

In many ways Irish conservationists have been marginalised as part of a process David Lloyd (1999, pp. 77, 79) describes as 'the subalternity effect'. Following on from Gramsci, Spivak and Homi Baba, Lloyd locates this effect within the contours of 'historiographical discourses' (*ibid.*) as part of the project of postcolonial cultural restructuring. From this perspective counter hegemonic cultural production can be attributed to these curators of heritage-based on 'non-elite histories: histories of agrarian movements, local histories, social histories of the complex intersections of class and colonisation in rural Ireland, women's history ... and social history' (*ibid.*). It is within this array of conservationists, archivists and antiquarians that we can find the curators of heritage, a disparate group who have rescued our heritage through vigilance and activism. For Tovey (1992, pp. 278, 280) the contestation of heritage in Ireland is an 'ideological conflict' (*ibid.*) with problems on all sides of the divide. For instance, the project of modernisation involves a debate about historically derived meanings surrounding built or natural environments. The demolition of Georgian Dublin was also part of a contested modernity (*ibid.*). Tovey quotes MacDonald's account of a government minister on the destruction of Georgian buildings in Kildare Street as claiming 'They stood for everything I hate' (Tovey, 1992, p. 279 from MacDonald, 1985, p. 12). The fact that much of Dublin's tenements were no more than slums in pre-independence Ireland added to the sense of ambivalence about the city's architectural heritage. Tourism has become marginalised in this development led economy, in an era when tourism has become part of 'the leisure industry' and part of 'the rural experience' (Marsden, Murdock, Lowe, Minton, & Flynn, 1993).

The state's own conservation plans have also drawn criticism from heritage advocates in recent years. Writing in *Heritage Outlook* (2000) Liam Lysaght called the Government Strategic Plan on forestry 'one of the greatest threats to our countryside' (Lysaght, 2000). The plantation of non-indigenous trees has become a contentious issue with serious consequences for landscapes and habitats. Local community infrastructure such as schools and health services has also had negative impacts on indigenous heritage.

THE SIGNIFICANCE OF ADVOCATES IN HERITAGE CAMPAIGNS

Without doubt, any attempt to mobilise collective responses to perceived threats to conservation or heritage sites requires the intervention of an advocate or interest group who contribute the levels of expertise necessary to bring a campaign together. In Ireland, heritage advocates have played a prominent role in Irish social and political life. Figures such as Mary Robinson, David Norris, Marian Finucane and Vincent Salafia have become national and international figures, and have gone on to become presidents and presidential candidates, senators and media presenters. Even that most outspoken of advocates Sir Bob Geldof has made a contribution to the heritage debate. 'Dublin is being savaged' he wrote in his introduction to Frank Mac Donald's book *Saving the City* (1989) 'with an almost methodological municipal vandalism'. For Geldof, progress through development was pointless if directed by 'the greedy, the corrupt, the stupid, the uninspired, the mediocre, the cheap, the tawdry, the vulgar-but mainly the indifferent' (*ibid.*). He felt the contempt visited upon Dublin's built heritage was similar to that displayed to its inhabitants who were corralled into a featureless suburbia, with its artists driven into exile.

MacDonald (1985, pp. 17, 19) has argued that the blame for much of Dublin's ills could be laid at the feet of rural and suburban developers, managers and planners who lacked sufficient empathy with their surroundings. Conversely, the same lack of empathy could be said to be characteristic of many planners and developers when dealing with rural conservation sites. Essentially, he has articulated an understanding of the need to see cities, towns and villages as living entities rather than commercial zones. In his books and editorials, MacDonald has consistently argued that planning and development needs to be undertaken with a sympathetic understanding of both place and hinterland, within an overall context which incorporates the history and ecology of an area. He remains a significant voice in Irish environmental and conservation circles, one who has had the vision to claim heritage as 'a cultural asset of immense importance' (*ibid.*). This understanding of the value of heritage is echoed in the discussion of 'the ideology of planning' (Harvey, 1985, pp. 165, 168). Here, a view of planning as an ideological process based on deterministic concepts of 'spatial ordering' (*ibid.*) is presented as part of a process of functionalist utility that promotes 'production, circulation, exchange and consumption' (*ibid.*) within a city or region. Seen from this perspective, planning must therefore reflect the concerns of the ruling social elite and their derivative interest groups and supporters. Nonetheless, heritage has an inherent value which shapes cultural expression. Our understanding of heritage as a source of contextual meaning has been informed by David Brett's (1996) discussion of heritage as 'a representation of the past' which provides an overall perception of how a nation 'views themselves and is viewed by others' (*ibid.*).

Heritage-based advocacy campaigns are invariably influenced by internal and external dynamics. Internal dynamics include the availability of aspects of economic, social and cultural capital (Bourdieu, 1986; Putnam, 2000), leadership and consensus building (Klandermans, 1989; Klandermans, Kriesi, & Tarrow, 1988) and the availability of empathetic professionals with appropriate levels of expertise (Leonard, 2005, 2006, 2008). The occurrence of structural re-arrangements in societies such as urbanisation and industrialisation promotes collective action as a result of perceived democratic deficits. While participation in new social movements is sometimes met with repressive measures from the authority of the state theorists such as Klandermans (1984) have developed the 'rational choice' theory which argues 'that the anticipated benefits outweigh the expected costs of participation'.

One response to this loss of local identity was the concept of 'rural development' which involved community-based initiatives to reinvigorate local discourse in the face of outside challenges, both culturally and environmentally speaking. A combination of grievances relating to depopulation, unemployment and neglect of rural regions provided successive environmental campaigns with a groundswell of dissent to facilitate mobilisation processes against multinationals or the political establishment. When combined with the renewed confidence achieved by new middle-class figures bolstered by expertise on rural rejuvenation programmes learned during migrant experiences abroad, a significant form of rural-based resistance emerged. This fundamental response came to be articulated around 'defence of space' types of territorial campaigns involving the imposition of industrial plants or infrastructural projects. Mick Smith argues that environmental citizenship now entails and that a much wider concept of ecological capital could be construed from 'culturally viable patterns of emotionally mediated responses' (Smith, 2005, p. 145) such as rural sentiment.

The outcome of this restructuring of the agricultural sector and increased reliance on multinational led development has been further ecological degradation, with Ireland facing fines for non-compliance on a series of European Union (EU) environmental directives. In addition, the state has applied the industrialisation approach to tourism. In the case of the Mullaghmore Interpretative Centre in County Clare on the west coast, the authority's plans to develop tourism through a series of visitors' centres across the island led to a significant campaign to protect the rare flora and fauna of the Burren in that County during the 1990s.[4] As the tourism industry developed it came to be associated with certain environmental impacts as the infrastructure of tourism – hotels, camping sites, holiday homes and marinas – began to dot the landscape. Further impacts were created from the increased road building, traffic and waste or sewage plants associated with such developments (Kousis, 2002, pp. 451, 452).[5]

One such 'gateway' chosen by the Office of Public Works (OPW) was Mullaghmore. It was the OPW's view that the interpretative centre should be located within the heart of the Burren rather than in a nearby village such as Corofin, to facilitate greater visual access for tourists in order to provide a 'first-hand experience of the park' (EIS Statement 1994 cited in McGrath, 1995, p. 57). The result of this decision would lead to a sometimes rancorous dispute which impacted on both sets of local groupings that were for or against the project, and lead to a series of legal challenges at national and European levels. The state's emphasis on an individualised consumer culture has led also to the commodification of transport, as public rail networks were allowed to diminish while private car ownership and motorways were prioritised. Over time, the focus on the Irish state's increased road building capacity has led to three significant anti-roads protests either side of the onset of the new Millennium.[6] All three protests emerged at a time when the state was attempting to develop the commuter hub around Dublin city. The case of Tara/Hill of Skryne would lead to a heated debate about the manner in which heritage is dealt within an age of rapid growth as the ancient site of Tara came under threat from the state's Critical Infrastructural Bill. This Bill which was introduced in the wake of a series of environmental campaigns has been seen by many as an attempt to prevent social movement-based collective responses in the future.

Similarly, the 'Shell to Sea' has raised conservation issues as part of their campaign of resistance to the Corrib gas pipeline. Protesters have raised concerns about ecological damage to local cliffs, drumlins and boglands as part of their campaign. The area surrounding the Rossport site is in line for designation as a Special Area of Conservation and Scenic Importance (Connolly & Lynch, 2005; Leonard, 2007). The state's own conservation plans have also drawn criticism from heritage advocates in recent years.[7] The plantation of non-indigenous trees has become a contentious issue with serious consequences for landscapes and habitats. Local community infrastructure such as schools and health services has also had negative impacts on indigenous heritage.

ECOPOPULISM AND IRISH CONSERVATION CAMPAIGNS

'Ecopopulism' – a term coined in 1994 by the American sociologist Andrew Szasz to describe the widespread, if not always closely coordinated, phenomenon of community groups coming together to protest against a variety of environmentally damaging threats – has long been a feature of Irish life. But in Ireland, more than in any countries, such conflicts take place in a context in which rural life and continuity with the past have historically been highly privileged. The exaltation of the peasant by the authors of early 1900s Literary Revival such as J. M. Synge and W. B. Yeats; the 'rural, Gaelic, and Catholic' ideology of the new nation; the construction of an idyllic image of Ireland by tourism promoters have all worked to sustain a prominent role for the rural dimension of Irish life. For many, changes in Ireland over the last half century reflect an ongoing disengagement from the traditional patterns of life that had embedded a set of values and practices that allowed rural communities to co-exist with their surrounding environment. The grievances of the wider population, which emerged from this perception of a loss of community, have contributed to the growth of populist environmentalism in Ireland, based on 'rural sentiment' – a collective resistance born of the community's inherent understanding of its place in the hinterland, away from the urban centre. During the pre-boom decades of the 1970s and 1980s, such ecopopulism was manifested within the rural-based discourse that characterised disputes over toxic substances and the activities of multinational disputes, among them lead and zinc mining at Tynagh, County Galway and gold mining near Croagh Patrick, the County Mayo site linked with St. Patrick (Leonard, 2007).

Some commentators have argued that the strong parochial rural sentiment contributes to the lack of acceptance of official environmental organisations in country-based disputes; as communities attempted to mobilise grievance based on local understandings and relationships, their concerns do not travel well. Such localism has also left many populist environmental groups open to the accusation of being merely cases of NIMBY – the familiar acronym for 'not in my back yard' – when opposition to industrial or infrastructural projects in a community's 'back yard', rather than in a larger systemic context, is identified as the primary rallying point for campaign mobilisation. Populist campaigns often face the problem of translating rural discourses into normal legal hearings. In the Rossport 5 campaign discussed below, for instance, local farmers' attempts to explain that it was unsafe to construct on bogland were simply not understood by those from outside the region, while to the locals building anything on a bog was patently unsustainable. Their point, rooted in rural experience, was reinforced when part of the bog and local cemetery washed away after being disturbed by the development of the refinery site. While specific populist environmental campaigns come and go, the significance of each campaign's contribution to an articulation of community grievance has created a movement of sorts, where outcomes can be measured through an understanding of the extent to which populist fundamentalism has come to be seen as the very basis for traditional rural identities in the post-consumption, post-modern era. The well of grievance that provides much of the underlying discontent for populist campaigns to exploit is the basis for an understanding of exactly how the various environmental campaigns that have occurred over recent decades can be characterised as components of an overall social movement. That movement constitutes part of the social capital of all rural and rural-urban communities. As such, it carries far greater significance than simply the impact of protest campaigns on policy implementation, such as the building of a pipeline, or the construction of a heritage centre in the middle of a Special Area of Conservation such as the Burren in County Clare. The impact of rural populist discourse goes beyond moments of access to political opportunity structures, and contributes to the shape and nature of the populist Irish political system itself.

Even before the recent economic downturn, communities in Ireland having enjoyed the benefits of extraordinary growth – the so-called Celtic Tiger – had also begun to witness the downside of the economic boom. Infrastructural projects had come to be perceived as threats to locals and their health and environment, or to the heritage of the nation itself. Such offshoots of rapid development as hyper-consumption, a buoyant property market, and increased car ownership led to further demand for roads, waste management sites and water treatment facilities. The link between growth and infrastructure was something of a sacred cow: Communities that voiced concerns about projects were widely deemed, in the press and in the statements of politicians, to be backward-thinking and against progress.

Throughout the boom years of the 1990s, Ireland had fallen foul of European directives on waste management due to an overreliance on landfill, which received up to 93% of the country's solid waste. The Irish Environmental Protection Agency was set up in 1992 to deal with such issues, but many critics charged that it quickly became associated with business interests and government appointments, rather than with environmental protection. To deal with the solid waste crisis, the government introduced plans for regional incinerators across the country. Previous attempts to introduce an all-island incinerator in Derry, Northern Ireland, were opposed by both nationalists and Unionists. Following on the networks created from the Northern campaign, communities mobilised in such regions as Galway, Cork and Meath and later, Dublin.[8] These regional campaigns benefited from links with the global anti-incinerator and 'zero-waste' campaigns, and from the support of experts from the United States and Britain. Communities began to inform themselves of the dangers posed by the dioxins and furans that are released into the air and food chain from incinerator emissions. The state's regional waste policy was seriously challenged by this campaign: One of the positive outcomes to community engagement with the waste issue was that regional recycling was introduced in many areas with great success.

The state has not abandoned its plans to introduce incinerators completely, as two major plants are still planned for Cork harbour and Poolbeg in Dublin; these will deal with the bulk of municipal and industrial waste. Only two years ago, the construction of housing – which had come to provide the second cycle of the Celtic Tiger boom – caused another environmental crisis, when the mass construction of new houses in rural areas led to the contamination of water supplies with effluent from archaic and suddenly overloaded treatment plants. Rural communities have borne much of the cost of Ireland's transition from an agrarian society into an industrialised, globalised economy, particularly in terms of environmental degradation and an undermining of significant aspects of heritage. The state's policy of prioritising rapid infrastructural development in order to underpin private consumption and multinational investment over local community services proved to be ill advised, leading to the economic collapse and IMF bailout of the late 1990s and 2000s.

Understanding of 'successful' outcomes for movements has been shaped by Gamson (1975) and Burnstein, Einwohner, and Hollander (1995) who have identified that 'realisation' and 'influence on policy' (state action) are the key factors in campaign impact assessment. These concepts have been further developed by Amenta and Caren (2004, p. 463) who have perceived the distinctions inherent between actual achievement of stated goals and the achievement of certain 'advantages for constituents'. Inevitably, movement success has therefore become synonymous with state acknowledgement and response to movement grievance. However, the subsequent achievement of aspects of a campaign's aims has also been recognised as a long-term result of collective action particularly when outcomes result from what Elias has termed 'unintended consequences' (Amenta & Caren, 2004,

p. 463). Changes to policy or adoption of movement aims as part of state policy can be part of this process. The formation of Irish environmental policy could be viewed as emerging in a dualistic response to bottom-up grassroots agitation on the one hand in addition to 'top down' EU legislation on the other. In the Irish case its populist political make-up lends itself to the attainment of some leverage for movements particularly at local level. However, the economic imperative of the state still dominates at policy level despite the occasional opening up of political opportunities at times of elections (Leonard, 2005).

THE FRAMING OF IRISH ENVIRONMENTAL CAMPAIGNS

We can apply this understanding of a discursive opportunity structure to the Irish environmental campaigns covered in this study in order to examine the consequences of this form of collective action. We can apply understandings of the types of protest, tactics, framing processes and outcomes to the different campaigns that have formed a part of the Irish environmental movements. A series of frames have been used by these movements including political, cultural, social, legal, institutional, economic, scientific and moral. Invariably the discursive framing patterns presented in cases of Irish environmental activism have emerged from a populist context.

Kitchings (1989) examines populism from the perspective of developing societies and makes the distinction between populism and neo-populism. While both are presented as critiques of industrialisation and mass-production in favour of small and localised entities 'populism' is defined as being based primarily in a social and ethical critique, whereas 'neo-populism' is seen as being 'more ambitious and 'not primarily oppositional' (Kitchings, 1989, pp. 20, 21). The process of migration from rural to urban centres during the industrial revolution is presented as a factor in the development of populism based on rural sentiment by Kitchings creating an 'anti-urban nostalgia' for the rural in elements of populism (*ibid.*). In the Irish context a left-leaning anti-capitalism and anti-militarism informed many of what have been termed 'first-phase' environmental disputes in Ireland (Leonard, 2005). This has been combined with a strong sense of identity that is grounded in rural discourse creating a strong sense of opposition to first phase, multinational projects in the 1970s and 1980s while contributing to the emergence of new middle-class opposition to 2nd phase state sponsored infrastructural projects in recent decades.

The initial campaign that came to define first phase disputes was the anti-nuclear protest at Carnsore Point. Campaign leaders were able to draw on existing moral and cultural frames in the process of creating a discursive response to plans for nuclear power in Ireland. The Carnsore Point protest benefited from wider symbiotic understandings of the perils of nuclear power created by United States and European anti-nuclear protestors in addition to the wider representation of the nuclear issue that were becoming part of popular culture. The linking of the Donegal uranium mining issue with the energy debates surrounding the state's plans for Carnsore brought together the anti-war and environmental camps at an early stage. However, while local populism played some role in the Tynagh Mines dispute the inability of the local population to create the momentum which would go beyond the economic rationale for mining at Tynagh contributed to the horrors that followed during the mining process and the scarred, poisoned site when it was eventually abandoned. The Tynagh Mines case and the subsequent degradation that occurred at the site and across its surrounding waterways and hinterlands should serve as a reminder to those who argue that communities should comply and take whatever economic benefits accrue from such acquiescence.

The one environmental campaign that can be seen as having a successful outcome for the movement involved was that of the Burren Action Group at Mullaghmore. Through a series of legal actions combined with a comprehensive understanding of the fragility of the Burren's eco-systems the BAG campaign achieved its goal of preventing tourist infrastructure from impinging on the Burren. It also contributed to an ongoing debate about the nature of heritage, identity and development both locally and internationally. The Mullaghmore campaign provides an illustration of the significance of expertise for any environmental group that finds itself in dispute with the interests of local authorities or the state.

The importance of new middle-class expertise has also been demonstrated as a key aspect of the anti-incinerator campaigns in Galway, Meath and Cork. The ability of these groups to contest the scientific data of the host industry or the state may not prevent incinerators being built in Ireland but this form of interest-led advocacy has informed concerned communities, industry and state officials about the potential risks of any incineration process that does not comply with strict processes of waste separation. In addition, the cultural importance of the reuse and recycle component of waste management has been reinforced by the anti-incineration campaigns, all of which presented recycling-led alternatives that would challenge the 'throw-away' syndrome so conspicuous in contemporary consumerism.

The debate about resources which first emerged in the 1970s and 1980s has resurfaced as part of the 'Shell to Sea' campaign. This campaign has reinvigorated the sense of community in Mayo and across rural Ireland, an identity that can be traced back to the agrarian agitation of the Land League. The territorial response of the North Mayo community to the perceived threats of the gas pipeline set to run across their lands is an instinctive one. The injustice surrounding the jailing of the 'Rossport 5' mobilised a wider response among the Irish populace which was growing angry at increased collusion between state and industrial interests at the expense of local communities.

The sense of grievance at state indifference to local or national heritage informs the anti-roads disputes. The current obsession with private car ownership over public transport has an ideological base. When combined with the destruction of heritage at Tara or Carrickmines or environmental degradation at the Glen of the Downs a new ideological response has emerged that draws on wider discursive challenges to articulate a coherent position based on a sense of environmental justice and conservation of the past.

CONCLUSION

The issue of conservation has never been satisfactorily resolved in the Irish case. The state's approach of supporting industries involved, alongside the seemingly reckless sell-off of our natural resources, led to a heightened sense of rural territorialism and a discursive process whereby communities reassessed their hinterlands when threatened by outside projects.

The Mullaghmore heritage dispute provides us with the best example of a campaign that achieved a successful outcome. The campaign led to a reversal of the state's plans to build an interpretative centre in the Burren. In addition, a wider debate about economic, social and cultural aspects of tourism and heritage was entered into by the supporters and opponents of the centre. When combined with the Burren Action Group's ecological expertise and ability to utilise national and European legal frameworks as sympathetic, discursive and strategic framing patterns were established which provided the campaigners with a successful outcome. Furthermore, national and international interest in the heritage and ecology of Ireland was rekindled. However, the dispute created a dichotomy between local groups opposed to or in favour of the interpretative centre and exposed tensions between local interests that favour economic environment over such interests.

Another framing issue for the new middle-class groupings was that of climate change. The framing process was extended in both the anti-incinerator and anti-roads movements to link the issues of toxic emissions and pollution from road usage as contributing aspects to the creation of greenhouse gases and climatic change. Although conservation campaigns only utilised the climate change frame in the wake of the popularisation of the subject in the wake of media debates surrounding the release of *An Inconvenient Truth*, such framing processes became an effective part of those campaign's tactical opposition and strategic approach, bring a level of perceived global scientific authority to localised protests, an approach which was picked up on by the media at the time.

The shift in policy direction undertaken by successive neo-liberal Irish governments led to a move towards a primarily ecological modernisation-orientated policy framework (as set out by the European Union). The emphasis on economic growth over environmental protection or concerns for communities has subsequently become a priority. This has been exacerbated by the Eurozone crisis and bailout of the Irish economy by the IMF since 2008.[9] Ultimately, the costs of economic growth have led to greater environmental degradation and an undermining of significant aspects of the nation's heritage. In particular, rural communities have borne the cost of Ireland's transition from a rural agrarian society into an industrialised and globalised economy. While communities have demonstrated a commitment to retaining some aspect of the traditional values and heritage of the 'Emerald Isle', the state's policy of prioritising rapid infrastructural development in order to underpin private consumption and multinational investment over local community services may prove to be ill advised as fluctuations on the global markets continue. As the cycle of the 'Celtic Tiger' gave way to the era of IMF sponsored austerity in the wake of the post-2008 economic crisis, the values and concerns of these local communities may provide a new direction for the post boom era.

NOTES

1. These disputes can be seen as part of an ongoing contestation of lifestyles and hinterlands in a society which has seen the economy shift from a situation where agriculture provided 10% of GNP in 1983 (representing 1 in 6 of the population) move down to 2.6% of GNP in 2006 (representing 1 in 20 of the population), according to press reports (*Irish Times* 15 February 2008).
2. Heffernan (1988, pp. 5, 6) discusses the events surrounding the Woodquay protests in detail.
3. Said argues that concepts of 'the Other' are used in the colonisation process. See Said, E. *Orientalism*. London: Penguin.
4. In an era characterised by high unemployment tourism was prioritised by the state as providing 10% of GNP with revenues of over IR£1,000 million (McGrath, 1995, p. 27).
5. Interpretative centres were seen as a necessary part of that infrastructural development in order that better understandings of Irish history and culture would be provided for visitors – 'creating interpretive "gateways" into our heritage' (O'Toole, 1994 from McGrath, 1995, p. 29).
6. These heritage campaigns occurred at the Glen of the Downs in County Wicklow, Carrickmines in County Dublin and at Tara/Hill of Skryne in County Meath (Leonard, 2008).
7. Writing in *Heritage Outlook* (2000) Liam Lysaght called the Government Strategic Plan on forestry 'one of the greatest threats to our countryside' (Lysaght, 2000).
8. These issues are discussed at length in Leonard (2011).
9. This is the subject of Leonard and Botetzagias (2011).

REFERENCES

Amente, E., & Caren, N. (2004). The legislative, organisational and beneficiary consequences of state orientated challenges. In D. Snow, A. Soule, & H. Kriesi (Eds.), *Blackwell companion to social movements*. London: Blackwell.

Bourdieu, P. (1986). The three forms of capital. In J. G. Richardson (Eds.), *Handbook of theory and research for the sociology of education* (pp. 241–258). New York, NY: Greenwood Press.

Brett, D. (1996). *The construction of heritage*. Cork: Cork University Press.

Burnstein, P., Einwohner, R., & Hollander, J. (1995). The success of political movements: A bargaining perspective. In C. Jenkins & J. Klandermans (Eds.), *The politics of grassroots environmental conflict*. New York, NY: St. Martin's Press.

Connolly, F., & Lynch, R. (2005). *The great Corrib gas controversy* (Vol. 1). Dublin: Centre for Public Inquiry.

Duncan, J. (1999). Elite landscapes as cultural (re)productions: The case of Shaugnessy Heights. In K. Anderson & F. Gale (Eds.), *Cultural geographies*. London: Longman.

Duncan, J., & Ley, D. (Eds.). (1993). *Place, culture and representation*. London: Routledge.

Gamson, W. (1975). *The strategy of social protest*. Belmont, CA: Wadsworth.

Harvey, D. (1985). *The urbanization of capital*. London: Basil Blackwell.

Heffernan, T. F. (1988). *Woodquay*. Austin, TX: University of Texas Press.

Irish Times. 15th February 2008.

Kitching, G. (1989). *Development and underdevelopment in historical perspective populism, nationalism and industrialisation*. London: Routledge.

Klandermans, B. (1984). Mobilization and participation in trade union action: An expectancy-value approach. *Journal of Occupational Psychology*, *57*(2).

Klandermans, B. (1989). *International social movement research. Organisation for change* (Vol. 2). Greenwich: JAI Press.

Klandermans, B., Kriesi, H., & Tarrow, S. (Eds). (1988). *From structure to action. International social movement research* (Vol. 1). Greenwich: JAI Press.

Kousis, M. (2002). Environmental impact of tourism. In J. Barry & E. G. Frankland (Eds.), *International encyclopedia of environmental politics*. London: Routledge.

Leonard, L. (2005). *Politics inflamed: GSE and the campaign against incineration in Ireland* (Vol. 1). In Ecopolitics Series. Drogheda: Choice Publishing.

Leonard, L. (2006). *Green nation: The Irish environmental movement from Carnsore Point to the Rossport 5* (Vol. 2). In Ecopolitics Series. Drogheda: Choice Publishing.

Leonard, L. (2007). The moral framing of a resource dispute. *Studies Irish quarterly review*. Dublin: Studies, Winter 2007.

Leonard, L. (2008). *The environmental movement in Ireland*. Dordrecht: Springer.

Leonard, L. (2011). Community campaigns for sustainable living: Health, waste and protest in civil society. Bingley: Emerald Group Publishing Limited.

Leonard, L., & Botetzagias, I. (Eds.). (2011). Sustainable politics and the crisis of the peripheries: Ireland and Greece (Vol. 8). In *Advances in ecopolitics*. Bingley: Emerald Group Publishing Limited.

Lloyd, D. (1999). *Ireland after history field day essays critical conditions*. Cork: Cork University Press.

Lysaght, L. (2000). *Heritage outlook* (Vol. 1). Dublin: The Heritage Council.

MacDonald, F. (1985). *The destruction of Dublin*. Dublin: Gill and MacMillan.

Marsden, T., Murdock, J., Lowe, P., Minton, R., & Flynn, A. (1993). *Constructing the countryside*. London: University College Press.

McGrath, B. (1995). *The mist-covered mountain: Change, conflict and identity in Ireland's countryside – The case of a planned development at Mullaghmore, Co. Clare*. Unpublished Masters Thesis. Galway: National University of Ireland Galway.

O'Toole, F. (1994). *Blackhole, greencard: The disappearance of Ireland*. Dublin: New Ireland Books.

Peace, A. (1997). *A time of reckoning: The politics of discourse in rural Ireland*. London: Routledge.

Pickvance, C. G., & Harloe, M. (1990). *Place, policy and politics: Do localities matter?* London: Routledge.

Putnam, D. (2000). *Bowling alone: The collapse and revival of American community*. New York, NY: Simon and Shuster.

Saunders, P. (1986). Reflections on the dual politics thesis: The arguments, its origins and its critics. In M. Goldsmith & S. Villadsen (Eds.), *Urban political theory*. Aldershot: Gower.

Smith, M. (2005). Citizens, Denizens and the *Res Publica*: Environmental ethics, structures of feeling and political expression. *Environmental Values, 14*.

Tovey, H. (1992). Environmentalism in Ireland. In P. Clancy, M. Kelly, J. Wiatr, & R. Zoltaniecki (Eds.), *Ireland and Poland: Comparative perspectives*. Dublin: UCD Press.

Tovey, H., Share, P., & Corcoran, M. (2007). *A sociology of Ireland* (2nd ed.). Dublin: Gill and MacMillan.

CHAPTER 4

WATER ☆

ABSTRACT

The issue of water supplies has been a significant one across all regions of Ireland in recent years. Both the years of growth and subsequent era of austerity since the Millennium have brought their own challenges and protests. This chapter will examine the issue of water supplies, taxes, infrastructure and community responses to state water policies.

Keywords: Water; charges; taxes; austerity; infrastructure

INTRODUCTION

Ireland, with her unspoiled scenery, clean water and fresh air, has traditionally been known as the 'Emerald Isle'. However, recent decades of rapid growth and unregulated development have jeopardised Ireland's natural resources. The 'Celtic Tiger' phase of accelerated growth which occurred in the Republic of Ireland had reached its peak in 2007. Over the previous decade, there had been an increase in crisis related to infrastructural development. While levels of personal wealth increased dramatically in the years leading up to 2007, the accompanying growth in consumption and waste also created a series of crisis and subsequent protests about water taxes, sewage treatment plants, landfills or planned incinerators, gas pipelines, roads, refuse collection and taxation, electricity pylons and mobile phone masts. As a member state of the European Union, Ireland had begun to implement an Environmental Modernisation based policy regime. Nonetheless, grassroots campaigns emerged from communities concerned about the health risks associated with accelerated development which threatened natural resources such as water supplies (Leonard, 2005, 2006).

☆ Part of this chapter has been published in Leonard (2013).

This chapter will be divided into various sections, reflecting the extent of Ireland's water crisis. The island of Ireland is divided into two jurisdictions: Northern Ireland, which is part of the United Kingdom; and the Republic of Ireland, which has its capital in the city of Dublin. The chapter will also present a case study on the water crisis that affected the western city of Galway in 2007. At various points since the 1990s, both man-made crisis emerging from poor planning and rapid development and flooding or freezing temperatures, which can be linked to climatic change, have impacted on water supplies in all parts of Ireland. In addition, the water charge protests are presented here. The relevant issues surrounding these cases will be discussed here, alongside a discussion of the environmental regulatory framework surrounding water provision in the Republic of Ireland.

WATER PROTESTS

According to the United Nations 'The right to safe and clean drinking water and sanitation as a human right that is essential for the full enjoyment of life and all human rights' (UN Resolution 64/292, July 2010). In the aftermath of Ireland's economic bailout by the IMF, successive governments have attempted to introduce a general water use taxation, despite the fact that the public already pays for such provisions in their tax. These water charges have been resisted across the country, and major protests have occurred nationwide, with the largest in Cork and Dublin. Over 10,000 people marched against water taxes in Dublin in April 2017. One of the main groups opposing the charges is the 'Right2Water' campaign. This group has organised many of the marches and protests across Ireland.

According to the state's water tax policy, Irish households will be charged for their water use, with the average charge for a household is expected to be about €240 per year, with regular increases expected. Previous to the introduction of this policy, all water services in Ireland were considered a public good and were paid for through general taxation, reducing the burden on the poorer in society. Protesters argue that the Irish state will also eventually privatise Irish Water. While those in favour of water charges argue that taxation will increase the conservation of domestic water supplies, those oppose feel it is associated with austerity and that savings could be made by improving Ireland's ageing water supply infrastructure. Fears of privatisation and the sell-off of water infrastructure resources also drive many to protest against water taxes. Protestors and those who refuse to pay the water charges have been hit with threats that their domestic water supply will be cut off.

Campaigners have also argued that private corporations will make water supplies a for profit venture, and both infrastructure and availability of clean water will be affected. The Right2Water campaign also argued that the move to privatisation would see a reduction of jobs with Irish Water, which would also have wider social and supply impacts. The campaign also made comparisons between this new 'water poverty' and fuel and food poverty which have impacted tens of thousands under harsh austerity measures. In addition, the protest group argued that the increase in water rates would hit the poorest, the elderly and the disabled disproportionately, while providing greater advantages for the corporate sector (right2water.ie).

THE BIG FREEZE

Ireland's water crisis has emerged as a serious threat to health across the island. In December 2010, thousands of residents in Northern Ireland were left without water due to freezing temperatures. Water supplies had to be sourced from neighbouring Scotland as pipes froze. The economic downturn had led to public sector water utility workers being laid off, and repairs to burst mains were severely hampered as a result. Officials from the Government-owned water supply company in Northern Ireland received 600,000 phone calls and were sent 10,000 emails while its website was bombarded by 500,000 hits during the worst week of the freeze. The Northern Ireland Water (NIW) chief executive subsequently resigned due to protests about the poor response to the crisis.

A similar situation faced citizens to the south in the Republic of Ireland, with water shortages becoming an annual problem in Dublin and surrounding counties, which are home to one-third of the nation's population. Record low temperatures created significant water shortages across the Republic of Ireland throughout December 2010 and early January 2011. Dublin City Council put water restrictions in place throughout the holiday season, with major implications for householders and businesses in the capital. A spokesman for the council said only half the amount of water necessary (about 20 million litres of water) was being saved each night during the freeze and subsequent thaw.

The daily demand at the Dublin reservoirs was around 507 million litres, 36 million litres fewer than was produced by the city's water treatment plants during the cold weather. Local authorities which are still implementing water supply provided standpipes or tankers for residents in the worst-affected areas, so people could collect water. Residents were reminded to bring their own containers and to boil all water collected before drinking. The Environment Department said they were satisfied with investment in water infrastructure. The Department claimed a water mains rehabilitation programme could be completed in 10 years if the current rate of investment continued.[1]

WATER SUPPLY IN IRELAND: A CONTESTED ISSUE

Domestic water charges have been introduced by government (through coalition minority partners the Green Party) in order to reduce domestic usage.

Plans to pipe water from Ireland's largest river, the Shannon, to alleviate Dublin's ongoing shortages have been met with resistance from conservationists and farmers who fear the long-term damage to the Shannon's water quality due to a proposal to extract over 300 million litres a day from one of the river's many areas of special conservation at Lough Ree in Ireland's midlands. According to conservationists, the planned 170 kilometre pipeline will lead to dramatically reduced water levels, as well as damaging vital tourist interests. One report by environmental scientists drew comparisons with the damage caused by water extraction at the Dead Sea in Israel:

> Many experts believe that a proposed rescue plan for the Dead Sea — pumping water from the Gulf of Aqaba in the Red Sea to replenish it — will only make matters worse. The rate of abstraction in the Red Sea project could mean that 1% of the sea's volume would be abstracted every 1,200 years. In the case of Lough Ree, the abstraction rate proposed by Dublin City Council would mean that 100% of the volume of the lake would be removed every five years. This can only lead to damaging and irreversible consequences at an alarmingly fast rate. (Business & Finance, 2007)

Ecological Modernisation and Irish Environmental Governance

After decades of economic stagnation, the Irish state embraced the dual agendas of neo-liberalism and neo-corporatist social partnership to create the economic basis for the multinational-led development that came to be synonymous with the boom decade of the 'Celtic Tiger'. In addition, the state prioritised unregulated infrastructural development as a response to the social needs of communities traditionally marginalised by high levels of unemployment and emigration. In many cases, planning was dealt with in a haphazard manner by the state and the industrial sector. As a result, vital infrastructure which had been neglected by the state over the decades before the 'Celtic Tiger' era of growth in the late 1990s was unable to cope with the post boom increase in demand, which has created many problems, including that of water provision (Leonard, 2013).

The resultant tension between environmental and developmental considerations creates a conflict where the state should mediate. However, in the Irish case, the demands of globalised industry have gained prevalence over that of the community due to neo-corporatist arrangements, with a series of regional crisis occurring as a result in recent years. This transition from policies aimed at providing services to those embedded industrial practice is reflected in the Irish environmental policy agendas. These policy frameworks had originally been devised in order to prevent pollution and regulate industry, but have subsequently come to facilitate corporations and economic growth. Much of this transition has been facilitated by the state's interpretation of the concept of ecological modernisation which underpins much of the environmental and developmental regulations in the Irish case (Leonard, 2013).

The threat to environmental purity has been a feature of the development rural areas hand as been a significant issue in contemporary Irish society. In the era of globalisation, Ireland's relationship with the European Union (EU) and the World Trade Agreement (WTA) has opened domestic markets through deregulation. For farmers and fishermen, the process of agriculture has become more expensive as global competition increased. An erosion of the traditional rural lifestyle, which included clean water supplies, has followed. New forms of globalised trade, tourism and development have created problems around the conservation and provision of resources like water, which is now an increasingly important national commodity. Affluence has also placed a strain on newly urbanised areas, as landfills and sewage treatment plants reach capacity in the wake of an economy which is driven by construction. Conservation has become a marginalised concept in this development led economy, with resultant impacts on the infrastructure which provides resources to communities.

Conservation issues in Ireland can be seen as part of a contest between two competing understandings of ecological modernisation – one is a technocratic form of green neo-liberalism, while the other is expressed by a grassroots engagement with green political economy. The most prevalent form of ecological modernisation is that which combines environmental and industrial concerns as a form of sustainable development. The ramifications for those wishing to adhere to green political economic thinking become clear in this process, as Ecological Modernisation (EM) creates a pro-industry rationale which then impacts upon the direction of parties in coalition. The influence of grassroots conservationists on maintaining an adherence to green political economic tenets is of considerable importance in areas such as water provision.

The response of the environmental movement sector resulted from the Irish state's pro-development, neo-liberal interpretation of the tenets of ecological modernisation, demonstrating the extent to which the state and industrial partners used their alliances in order to overcome local concerns about resources and commonage. The shift in the state's policy direction undertaken by successive neo-liberal Irish governments has led to increased conflict between communities and the state in relation to infrastructural projects and development (Leonard, 2008). While the Irish state has attempted to follow the ecological modernisation policy framework set out by the European Union, the emphasis is on economic growth over environmental protection or concerns for communities. Ultimately, the costs of economic growth have led to greater environmental degradation and an undermining of significant aspects of the nation's resources, including its water supply.

What becomes clear is the degree to which local factors in Ireland such as alliances between the political sector and property speculators which fund these parties lead to an ideological shift in the state's responses to EU derived policy or directives. In this way, the Irish state can be seen to lack core 'green' values within its wider policy framework, unlike other countries. Environmental values and state imperatives reached congruence at various stages of each states' development of environmental policy frameworks and movement activism over recent decades, with EM becoming central to either wider acceptance of environmental initiatives in the case of Germany or becoming part of the ecomodernist versus ecopopulist divide in the case of the United States, which an old fashioned stand-off between economy and environment still exists. To an extent, his dichotomy between the economically derived imperative of the state and the sub-politics of conservationist movements exists in Ireland. While undoubtedly eco-modernism has provided an outlet for the many competing elements in the Irish environmental arena and it has crystallised current understanding of what the environmental protection means from an industry perspective, it is not without its criticisms. Although facilitating policy making at an administrative level and bringing diverse elements of pollution control together under holistic regulatory frameworks, eco-modernism has been criticised for being too inclined towards industry for an ecologically minded concept. This criticism may overlook the necessary role of ecological modernisation in bridging the gap between the state, industry and the environment, in the face of the regulatory failure of the past.

The impact of neo-liberalism on ecological modernisation in the Irish case becomes evident when we note the manner in which successive Irish governments attract multinationals for the purpose of job creation. In the event of environmental regulations hampering the operation they may often be altered or overlooked and in the easing of conflicts of interests, the public is often caught in a propaganda war over the merits of industrial progress in relation to environmental protection. A feature of this debate is the conflict between the public relations section of the polluting industry, which was given practically limitless funding to give their viewpoint and the oppositional efforts of concerned citizens and groups who had little or no previous expertise and no funding beyond public contributions. Ireland has followed a neo-liberal plan for growth that has overridden environmental concerns and subsequently impacted on water supplies. In order to address resultant problems, new legislation has been enacted (Leonard, 2013).

DRINKING WATER LEGISLATION IN IRELAND

Ireland's drinking water is protected under both European Union and national legislation. The Water Services Act 2007 prioritises the protection of human and public health. The European Union Drinking Water Directive (98/83/EC of 3 November 1998) set standards for the most common substances in Irish drinking water.[2] Where the water quality does not meet the specified standards, remedial measures are outlined. These regulations do not change the monitoring requirements or water quality standards (except for fluoride), from previous regulations but do change the enforcement of the regulations, assigning new powers to the Environmental Protection Agency (EPA) and Local Authorities, and explicitly refer to the role of the HSE in relation to both the water supplier and the supervisory authority. Consultation with and agreement of the HSE are required where there are implications for public health. Failure of the water supplier to comply with specific aspects of the regulations is an offence and prosecution may be taken by the supervisory authority. The main provisions of these regulations from HSE perspective are outlined as Protection of human health, Supervisory authority, Notification of consumers, Monitoring and Protection of Human Health.

The Authority works with the HSE during any crisis to provide actions or notice in the following manner:

a. The supply of such water is prohibited, or the use of such water is restricted, or such other action is taken as is necessary to protect human health,
b. Consumers are informed promptly thereof and given the necessary advice, and
c. In the case of a public water supply, the Agency (EPA) is informed promptly (http://www.hse.ie).

The responsibility for the provision of safe drinking water rests with the Local Authorities, while other agencies that are involved include the Department of the Environment, Heritage and Local Government, the EPA and the HSE. Respective roles and responsibilities are described below. Water Services Authorities made up of 29 County Councils and five City Councils are responsible for the quality of drinking water, and the councils must work with the health authority where there are health concerns with the supply.

While the EPA has supervisory authority over the Water Services Authorities concerning the quality of the drinking water, the Water Services Authorities maintain direct supervisory authority over the providers of other water supplies, such as private group schemes in rural areas and other private supplies. The Water Services Authority also ensures that the water supplies that come under the regulations are monitored at the frequency provided for in the Drinking Water Regulations. This monitoring service provided jointly through the Environmental Health Service (HSE) and the HSE laboratories in conjunction with Water Services Authorities laboratories with a combination of monitoring procedures in place in certain geographic regions. In 2007, one such region, Galway city and county, suffered a major water crisis, with an ensuing health crisis due to a parasite in municipal supplies.

THE GALWAY WATER CRISIS

In recent years, water legislation has been accompanied by the threat of water charges being levied on Irish householders. A number of community groups have protested against charges. Nonetheless, Irish drinking water had been supplied with relatively few problems until the property construction boom of the late 2000s. European and national legislation was implemented regional by the relevant local councils. However, in the case of the *cryptosporidium* outbreak in the western Irish city of Galway in the spring of 2007, a 'blame game' of accusation and counter accusation broke out between the various layers of institutional politics involved in the provision of municipal water to the city and its environs.

The issue of water pollution in the Irish case can be traced back some time before the current crisis emerged. The water crisis issue can be understood as a contestation between various forms of expertise. In the Galway case, local and national experts from a diverse range of fields made contributions to the water quality debate. These groups were comprised of scientific experts, politicians, planners and civic groups.[3] Local fishermen provide an example of one such group who provided an element of local expertise to the wider contested debate. Anglers on Lough Corrib have had long standing concerns about water quality, while scientists attempted to raise the issue as far back as 1997 when the *Geological Survey of Ireland* first highlighted a cryptosporidium risk for the Galway region due to the absence of soil layers prevalent in other parts of the country. In the west, the indigenous karst limestone topography provided little in the way of the filtering effect necessary to break down micro-organisms such as cryptosporidium, increasing the risk of water contamination (*ibid.*).

The central issue of the 'water crisis' was manifested through the infestation of local water supplies with the cryptosporidium parasite in the wake of a series of floods, which was compounded by years of poor urban and rural infrastructural development. The cryptosporidium parasite is a microscopic parasite which becomes attached to the human intestine when ingested. It results in cramps and diarrhoea for most people, with severe cases of infection in very young or old people leading to severe illness and in a few reported cases, even death. The key source of the bug is both animal and human waste, with any infestation of water supplies usually being attributed to waste appearing in the water supply at some point (*Irish Times*, 2007).

In the case of Lough Corrib, the largest lake in the Republic, effluence from large tracts of counties Mayo and Galway is washed through the lake and into the water supply for most of the local population, including the 70,000 inhabitants of Galway City. Towns surrounding Lough Corrib and its tributaries have become part of the bourgeoning commuter belt around the prosperous city of Galway, enticed by the promise of profit from selling up in the city which is second only to Dublin in second hand property prices. As a result, sprawling housing developments have sprung up around all of the towns near Galway city, replicating the inflated national property market which has been synonymous with the second phase of the 'Celtic Tiger' once its original determinant of multinational investment had subsided as global economies began to contract (Leonard, 2013).

The issue of rapid development and subsequent social harms and environmental degradation can be applied to the Irish case through understandings of environmental sociology (Hannigan, 2006) and risk society (Beck, 1992; Giddens, 1999). The extent of the organisation of Irish society around risks such as rapid development on flood plains during the construction boom of the 1990s, as Irish society became preoccupied with risks and harms such as flooding on an extensive scale. The onset of 'risk society' in the Republic of Ireland has been a characteristic of the 'Celtic Tiger' years of growth, as a predominately rural society came to be transformed into a modern European state that urbanised rapidly in two decades (Leonard, 2008, 2009). This 'manufactured risk' stemming from human activity such as poor planning and development practices is compounded when the political system is influenced by links between property developers and mainstream political parties, particularly when this relationship comes under the scrutiny of successive Tribunals of Inquiry, as has happened in the Irish case. According to Kirby, this represents 'the enrichment of an elite and the marginalisation of … citizens from the benefits of economic growth' (Kirby, 2006, p. 181; cf. Leonard, 2009, p. 280).

The fact that Galway had maintained its multinational presence through large multinational employers meant that a steady flow of people continued to be attracted to this western where its two-third level institutions and culturally rich reputation provided Galway with the reputation of a dynamic young and growing city. In March 2007, news began to spread of a contamination threat to the city's water supply. Tests by the Health Service Executive (HSE) were conducted across the city and county as the extent of the problem began to emerge. Residents in the city and surrounding areas were promptly advised to boil all drinking water until notified otherwise. Panic buying of bottled water was reported over the bank holiday weekend as hotels, bars and restaurants struggled with the influx of tourists for the traditional St. Patrick's Day festival.

The boil notice was announced as a precaution while the authorities searched for the source of the outbreak. Testing was initially concentrated at the city's ageing waterworks which were first constructed in the late 1940s with a second facility being built in 1972. Most municipal waterworks contain the cryptosporidium parasite through a filter system. However, the older Galway facility had a simple mesh to remove large pieces of waste, followed by a process of chlorination which in itself doesn't kill the cryptosporidium. The local council was aware of a significant risk of cryptosporidium from 2005 (Irish Times, April 14, 2007). This news was enough to engender an immediate response from the government, particularly in an election year. The government was concerned about damage to tourism as much as the health of its citizens, and tried to pass off the blame for the issue on the elected representatives of Galway's local authority.[4]

One issue that was clarified by the tests conducted by public health scientists was that the source of the crisis was human rather than animal waste. This confirmed the fact that unregulated development had been the cause of the water contamination due to the insufficient waste treatment plants in areas that had been overdeveloped along Lough Corrib, the largest lake in the Republic which flowed by river into Galway Bay and the Atlantic Ocean. However, for the beleaguered citizens of Galway, the cause of the crisis was of much less significance than the solution. Within weeks of the crisis, a populist community movement was mobilised in response to the issue.

Representatives of a local group which was protesting about the health risks of the Galway Water Crisis in their campaign stated that the campaigners as a group felt 'let down' by both local and national politicians who 'seemed more interested in passing the blame than actually doing anything about this crisis'. A letter from the group continued by stating that the state was taking one and a half million euros a week in taxes for water sales, and that the group wanted that money used in the efforts to solve the crisis. Some local authority councillors criticised the proposed use of UV technology, stating that ultra violet tubes were less efficient in water which had darkened with a tint, as the contaminated water in the Corrib had due to pollution (Leonard, 2013).

In addition, he claimed that while UV light worked with most microbes, it wasn't effective on protozoa such as the cryptosporidium. The councillors suggested a Russian method of electrochemically activated water or anolyte, which was a non-toxic way of destroying all microbes effectively. Politically, successive environmental campaigns have strengthened the responses of civil society from the grassroots up, bolstering pluralistic discourses at a time when that aspect of democracy has come under threat from a variety of sources including an increasingly technocratic state and a body-politic damaged by a series of planning related scandals.

Environmental social movements have benefited mainstream politics in Ireland as witnessed by the rise of the Green party in local, national and European elections over recent decades. One distinctive outcome of environmental conflict has been the establishment of the Environmental Protection Agency (EPA) in 1992. The EPA was originally criticised for its location of a regulatory framework within the context of the state's industrial development policies but the agency has come into its own over time and is now a leading component of institutional environmentalism in Ireland spanning a range of ecological, educational and regulatory responses. However, some distance remains between the EPA and many grassroots campaigns such as those campaigning for clean water and the bridging of this gap remains an outstanding issue for all levels of environmentalism in the Irish case.

The response of the political sector was one of passing blame for the crisis. Local politicians claimed the crisis arose as a result of 'a government which was seen to be overtly focused on speculative development'. The political sector was already being blamed for poor planning in relation to Galway's sewage treatment plant, which was built in Galway Bay with a large investment from the European Union in the mid-1990s, only to reach capacity with a couple of years due to the explosion in home and industrial construction in a city sometimes called 'the fasting growing city in Europe' (Leonard, 2013).

Others felt that culpability rested with a number of groups such as the HSE, the city and county managers, the elected councillors, the Department of the Environment and the Environmental Protection Agency. Commentators stated that risk assessment procedures were not carried out properly over many years, and that the exceptionally heavy rainfall and subsequent flooding which had occurred in Galway that winter should have alerted the authorities to the need to monitor the water supply for problems (author date). One editorial claimed that gallons of raw sewage were being pumped into the rivers and lakes of Galway, as well as Galway Bay due to new housing developments.

For their part, Galway city managers claimed that the water crisis would end on June 15 with the increase in supply of clean water from a nearby plant. The council also had plans to repair water pipes in the city. However, with the General election taking place at the end of May, the local media began to speculate as to which candidate would be most affected by the water crisis. The issue had relegated all others to secondary importance, becoming major issue in the Galway West electoral constituency during the 2007 national elections.[5]

The Galway Water Crisis campaign had mobilised large levels of public anger which was now being directed at public officials due to the crisis. Speculation began to emerge as to which of the city candidates in the forthcoming national elections would be most affected by the water crisis. Local politicians also had to contend with the protest campaign of the 'Galway Water Crisis' group. The group claimed that public faith in the political system had been 'irreparably damaged' by the water crisis. Many felt that the risk of an outbreak of cryptosporidium even after a new plant was built would remain, due to poor monitoring and unregulated development, according to the group:

> The feedback we are getting from the public is that they would be afraid to drink the water from the city system again. Unless we tackle the major problem of cleaning Lough Corrib, then this problem will simply come back again and again. (*ibid.*)

The campaign claimed that the problem was one which affected all the towns around Lough Corrib, not just the city areas reliant on the old Terryland plant. These areas had unreliable sewage systems which pumped effluent into the Lough. For the campaigners, 'the major problem lies with the cleaning of the Corrib. There will always be a problem as long as raw sewage is coming into the Lough' (*ibid.*). The water campaign brought its protest to a meeting of Galway City council, calling for 'Clean Water for Galway'. Protesters brought their empty water bottles to deposit at City Hall as part of their protest, to highlight the rising cost for citizens having to buy water and recycle bottles, in a city which ironically had led the way when recycling pilot schemes had been first introduced (Leonard, 2005). The water campaign's webpage had nearly 1,000 hits in its first two weeks, indicating the lack of information available from official sources for citizens concerned about the health risks of the water crisis in Galway.

Local politicians called for localised filtering systems so people could collect free water. They claimed that the Government had plans to privatise water supplies across Ireland, something which led to the delay in 'the allocation of EU and state funds for water and sewage services to local authorities' (Irish Times, April 24, 2007). These elected representatives also pointed out that while citizens faced payment of large fines from the European Union due to the non-implementation of European Union Directives, they were also being denied clean water due to 'government failure' (Galway Independent, 25 April, 2007). The Mayor did receive some support from the Heritage Group *An Taisce* who claimed that the construction of new housing should be frozen until the water crisis was sorted out. This moratorium should remain in place until 'the essentials of life' such as good drinking water, sewage treatment and waste disposal systems were sorted out (*ibid.*).

The outcome of this issue can be understood when viewing the water crisis as an example of societal risk borne from poor planning practices. From a social movement theory perspective, the crisis is indicative of the difficulties faced by campaigns and key activists alike when electoral success deprives movements of their potential leadership group. The experience of activists who became part of the city council in Galway demonstrates the difficulties for campaigners who become 'cut off from the activist base' (Leonard, 2008). The problem of cooptation for activists who embrace the political mainstream remains an outstanding obstacle for those environmental advocates now faced with negotiating with a government which included a Green Party Minister for the Environment.

The beleaguered citizens of Galway had little respite through the economically important summer festival season. The HSE's announced that up to 238 cases of cryptosporidiosis had been recorded in Galway in 2007, with non-reported cases estimated in much higher numbers. The boil notice was lifted in east Galway in July, due to the extension of services from the revitalised water plant in the city (Galway Advertiser, July 21, 2007). The famous Galway Race Festival was declared 'cryptosporidium free' due to a 100,000 euro investment in water filters at the local race course. Commercial interests, which had complained of losses during the tourist season, were offered a 10% rate rebate.

In 2007, nearly a quarter of a million lost water supplies in the south western region of England due to extreme flooding, while other regional Irish towns such as Ennis and Clonmel were also hit with boil notices due to flooding. For Galway's local authorities, the loss of confidence from the public in its services was equalled by costs of over 400,000 euros in weekly laboratory tests at its water plants. After a series of delays, water supplies to the city and its western environs were returned to Galway city as the last obstacles to providing acceptable levels of clean water from the revitalised local plant to the city were overcome (with supply rising from 14,000 m^3 of water to 17,000 m^3), according to Galway's City Manager (Galway City Tribune, July 13, 2007). With cryptosporidiosis cases dwindling to pre-crisis levels, the Galway water debacle was coming to an end. Water supplies were restored on August 20. The final bill for the Galway crisis was set at 15 million euros, including the costs to industry and private households (Connacht Sentinel, August 21, 2007). In 2008, Galway would be beset by further water problems as lead corrosion began to effect local water supplies with a new risk, leaving householders reaching for theory water drums again.

RESPONSE TO THE WATER CRISIS

Ireland's water crisis has led to a crisis of what Bourdieu (1986) has called 'governmentality', as various state and regional bodies compete for ascendancy over the nation's water supply. Department of the Environment response was to ensure water bodies in the country met strict criteria to be set out soon in the EU's Water Framework Directive. Local authorities have huge challenges ahead if Ireland is to avoid fines and worse, with 85% of water bodies at risk of not meeting the objectives. EPA experts had long harboured concerns about the type of water crisis experienced in Galway, but their concerns were ignored during the property development led economic boom, which ran from 1998 through to 2006.

The cryptosporidium issue was believed to have arisen because one of Galway's two water treatment plants was not capable of removing the faeces-borne parasite and other pathogens from the water supply, according to the EPA. The EPA also feared many of Ireland's other regional water supplies, and many treatment plants serving the 900 public water supplies across the country are under threat from a similar crisis to Galway, particularly in an era of climate change-related flooding. An EPA report found that one in five plants were either high-risk or very high-risk out of a survey of half of the nation's facilities

Water shortages are another concern, due to a rapidly aging supply system. The greater Dublin area system, which delivers 520 million litres of drinking water everyday to the city and surrounding counties, faces serious stresses from a growing demand which was never planned for in the boom years. Pipe leakage has increased by 30 million litres a night at the height of 2010s big freeze. Daily demand in the summer can see increases of up to 40 million litres. While plans have been set for an improvement to the municipal pipe system, the fact remains that Dublin runs the serious risk of having supply outstrip demand.

MacDonald (1989) has argued that the blame for much of Dublin's ills could be laid at the feet of rural and suburban developers, managers and planners who lacked sufficient empathy with their surroundings. Conversely, the same lack of empathy could be said to be characteristic of many planners and developers when dealing with rural conservation sites. Essentially, he has articulated an understanding of the need to see cities, towns and villages as living entities rather than commercial zones. In his books and editorials, MacDonald has consistently argued that planning and development needs to be undertaken with a sympathetic understanding of both place and hinterland, within an overall context which incorporates the history and ecology of an area.

MacDonald's view of planning as an ideological process is based on deterministic concepts of 'spatial ordering' which is presented as part of a process of functionalist utility that promotes equity in the production, supply and consumption of vital resources such as water within a city or region. Seen from this perspective, planning must therefore reflect the concerns of the ruling social elite and their derivative interest groups and supporters. At the heart of this equation is a capitalism which promotes private property and free market industry as two of its main tenants, foregoing other concerns about equity of distribution.

Ireland has a natural imbalance in its distribution of water. According to the EPA, there are about 76,000 litres of water per capita per day available in the west of Ireland and about one-tenth of that, 7,600 litres of water per capita per day, in the greater Dublin region. Climate change has caused further problems for the supply of water on the island, with the EPA reporting in 2009 that the implications of climate change will have serious results on both the availability and subsequently, the quality, of Ireland's domestic water supply. The state will be forced to arbitrate between competing industrial, agricultural and householder demands for water as a result.

Water supplies will be reduced in the east by up to 40%, with most water emanating in low lying areas which provides surface water that is more exposed to climatic-related issues such as flooding. Further concerns have arisen due to the ongoing rise in global temperatures, which will affect nation's water supplies globally. Even a rise of one percent can lead to reductions in rainfall due to droughts. The supply to both new housing developments and industries in the east has reached its limits as the same bodies of water are used for the cooling of high-tech equipment, domestic drinking and effluence, a contest which seems to have evaded planners during the era of rapid development. These issues have been exacerbated by the problem of increased pollution.

The Irish state has included plans to develop water infrastructure by five billion euros. However, these plans are now under threat due to the nation's economic collapse and subsequent EU/IMF fiscal bailout. Many large scale development projects have been put on hold as a result. The state plans to introduce water meters, but needs to survey and repair the country's entire supply infrastructure before this can be achieved, a large scale project which is also facing delays due to fiscal constraints.

GOVERNANCE IMPLICATIONS: THE WATER FRAMEWORK DIRECTIVE

The EU Water Framework Directive is an important piece of EU environmental legislation which aims at improving our water environment. It requires governments to take a new holistic approach to managing their waters. It applies to rivers, lakes, groundwater, estuaries and coastal waters. Member States must aim to achieve good status in all waters by 2015 and must ensure that status does not deteriorate in any waters. This website is an information resource for interested parties and holds extensive documentation relating to WFD-related studies and River Basin Management Plans. National regulations implementing the national Water Framework Directive (WFD) were introduced in 2003. The objectives of the Water Framework Directive are 'to protect all high status waters, prevent further deterioration of all waters and to restore degraded surface and ground waters to good status by 2015'. A major programme is under way to achieve this somewhat ambitious target. In the aftermath of the introduction of the Water Framework Directive (WFD), water policy and protection has been devolved from European or national governance levels down to the community level.

New regulations were introduced for the establishment of seven Water Advisory Councils around the country, one in each River Basin District (RBD), as part of an integrated approach to water management under the WFD, providing communities with a role in the management of local water supplies and amenities. The objectives of the Water Framework Directive (WFD) are to protect all high status waters, prevent further deterioration of all waters and to restore degraded surface and ground waters to good status by 2015. National regulations implementing the directive have been put in place in 2003. The Environmental Protection Agency (EPA), Department of the Environment, Heritage and Local Government, local authorities and associated consultancies prepared the Article 5 Characterisation Report for the Irish River Basin Districts. This was submitted to the EU in Brussels in November 2004 (http://www.epa.ie/whatwedo/wfd/).

CONCLUSION

Ireland is coping, albeit with some difficulties, to provide municipal water supplies to its population. Annual water demand in Ireland has been projected to increase by 76,707 million litres by 2015. The National Urban Wastewater Study concluded that 48% of the wastewater treatment plants in Ireland would be adequate to treat future projected loadings in year 2022. 85% of wastewater treatment plants studied in 2002 currently limits discharges to meet environmental quality objectives in the receiving waters. The cost of water services are projected to increase by 75% by 2015.

As we have seen, the results of poor planning have been shouldered by local communities across Ireland Drinking water supplies was contaminated with the cryptosporidium virus. Lax regulation of the construction industry by the state created a growing strain on the city's water and sewage systems, and after heavy flooding in 2007 and 2008, water supplies in Lough Corrib which supplied Galway city and other towns became contaminated. The water crisis also became an issue during the general election of May 2007, and was said by some commentators to have cost the city's Green Party Mayor a seat in the Dublin parliament. Despite this crisis, Ireland was again plunged into crisis in the winter of 2010, when freezing temperatures led to tens of thousands of residents losing water supplies over the holiday period. The austerity years since the IMF bailout has led to the introduction of water charges, which have been resisted by communities across Ireland.

However, with reports of increased instances of extreme weather forecast by the United Nations World Meteorological Organisation (WMO) after a decade when extreme weather events occurred in a 'range which is well outside the historical norm' (Irish Times, August 9, 2007), the threat of instances of flood related water contamination will remain for communities in Ireland and across the planet. With poor infrastructure and increased fiscal constraints in the aftermath of the Ireland's economic bailout by the European Union and International Monetary Fund, citizens across Ireland will be hoping for a sustained and effective response from their political leaders to address this issue before another water crisis occurs, particularly in the heavily populated east coast.

NOTES

1. *Irish Times*, January 4, 2011.
2. These standards were translated into Irish law by the European Communities (Drinking Water) (No. 2) Regulations 2007 (S.I. No. 278 of 2007). The European Communities (Drinking Water) (No. 2) Regulations 2007 (S.I. No. 278 of 2007) prescribe the quality standards to be applied.
3. For a detailed account of civil society mobilisations on ecological issues in Galway, see Leonard (2005) *Politics Inflamed.*
4. For a more in-depth account of the issue of 'contested notions of sustainable rural tourism' in the Irish case, see McArevey, McDonough, and Heneghan (2009).
5. One election candidate stated that the issue was being raised on 'at least 50% of all doors we canvass' (*Galway Advertiser*, April 26, 2007).

REFERENCES

Beck, U. (1992). *Risk society: Towards a new modernity.* London: Sage.

Bourdieu, P. (1986). The three forms of capital. In J. G. Richardson (Ed.). *Handbook of theory and research for the sociology of education* (pp. 241–258). New York, NY: Greenwood Press.

Business and Finance Magazine. (2007). Ireland's Water Crisis. 43(8), Dublin: Moranna.

Connacht Sentinel August 21 2007.

Galway Advertiser April 26 2007.

Galway Advertiser July 21 2007.

Galway City Tribune July 13 2007.

Galway Independent April 25 2007.

Giddens, A. (1999). Risk and responsibility. *Modern Law Review*, *62*(1), 1–10.

Hannigan, J. (2006). *Environmental sociology: A social constructivist perspective.* London: Routledge.

Irish Times April 14 2007.

Irish Times April 24 2007.
Irish Times August 9 2007.
Irish Times January 4 2011.
Kirby, P. (2006). Bringing social inclusion to the centre: Towards a project of active citizenship. In D. Jacobsen, P. Kirby, & D. Ó. Broin (Eds.), *Taming the Celtic tiger: Social exclusion in a globalised Ireland* (pp. 180–199). Dublin: New Ireland.
Leonard, L. (2005). *Politics inflamed: GSE & the campaign against incineration in Ireland* (Vol. 1). In Greenhouse Press Ecopolitics Series. Drogheda: Choice.
Leonard, L. (2006). *Green nation: The Irish environmental movement from Carnsore Point to the Rossport* 5 (Vol. 2). In Greenhouse Press Ecopolitics Series. Drogheda: Choice.
Leonard, L. (2008). *The environmental movement in Ireland*. Dordrecht: Springer.
Leonard, L. (2009). Social partnership's boiling point: Environmental issues and social responses to neo-liberal policy in Ireland. *Critical Social Policy*, *29*(2), 279–293.
Leonard, L. (2013). The water crisis in Ireland: The socio-political contexts of risk in contemporary society. In J. R. Wagner (Eds.), *The social life of water*. New York, NY: Berghahn Press.
MacDonald, F. (1989). *Saving our city: How to halt the destruction of Dublin*. Dublin: Tomar.
McArevey, R., McDonough, J., & Heneghan, M. (2009). Conflict to consensus: Contested notions of sustainable rural tourism on the Island of Ireland. In J. McDonough, T. Varley, & S. Shortall (Eds.), *A living countryside?: The politics of sustainable development in Ireland*. Aldershot: Ashgate.
The National Urban Wastewater Study. Retrieved from www.wfdireland.ie. Accessed on December 21, 2010.

Websites

www.rte.ie April 29 2007
www.myspace.com/galwaywatercrisis
http://www.epa.ie/whatwedo/wfd/
http://www.right2water.ie/

CHAPTER 5

RESOURCES☆

ABSTRACT

This chapter will examine the response of a rural community in Ireland to the imposition of a gas pipeline on their farms, in the western coastal county of Mayo. This analysis will include a discussion of the concept of 'rural community sentiment' (Leonard, 2006, 2008a, 2008b) as a factor in the mobilisation of community campaigns against infrastructural projects which are perceived as a threat to existing ways of life in regional areas. The chapter will also explore key theoretical concepts for this community-based responses to environmental degradation in rural areas, including critical criminology and rural criminology, resource curse theory and ask whether the campaign was ecopopulist, with issues of social and environmental justice at its core. This will be achieved through a case study approach. In so doing, the chapter will highlight the basis for rural community's campaigns of opposition to development projects imposed by corporate or state bodies in the Irish case.

Keywords: Rural community; rural sentiment; gas pipeline; corporate projects; development; mobilisation

INTRODUCTION

Land grabbing is described as a process involving 'outsiders – nation-states as well as corporations – colluding with local domestic elites to radically alter existing land ownership and land uses' (White, 2014, p. 1). This chapter will examine one such process, which pitted a rural Irish community against corporate actors and state agencies in an attempt to protect their families and land from the imposition of an onshore gas pipeline and processing plant. This form of dispute has been demonstrated to have 'social justice issues' at its core (Carrington & Perira, 2011). This campaign of opposition would lead to the

☆Part of this chapter was published in Leonard (2008b).

imprisonment of local activists, known as 'the Rossport 5', the establishment of an activist community group ('Shell to Sea') which was opposed to the ecological degradation caused by the pipeline in an area which had been set out as a conservation area due to its scenic beauty and biodiversity. The chapter utilises White's understanding of 'activity which diminishes social equity in the provision of healthy sustainable environments' (White, 2014, p. 1) as 'eco-crime' in order to locate this case within the rural criminology/green criminology nexus.

The chapter's framework incorporates a number of competing actors, each of which takes a position on the pipeline project based on their dominant paradigms. For the corporate entities (Royal Dutch Shell and Norway's Statoil), the development represents an opportunity for profit making from resources embedded in the North Atlantic off the Irish coastline. The Irish state was promoting a form of accelerated development which would bring jobs to rural areas. Although agriculture and fishing had traditionally provided employment for some in the local community, emigration rates remained high in the region. The state was committed to the introduction of large-scale infrastructural projects as part of the prevailing neo-liberal policies favoured by the coalition government which was in power from the earliest days of this pipeline dispute, through to the economic crisis which followed the collapse of the Irish banking system in 2008. In addition, a coalition of groups opposed to the pipeline emerged in support of the local farmers who were imprisoned for refusing to sign a document in which they would guarantee to stay away from the pipeline, despite its proximity or incursion on to their lands.

This dispute occurred in line with a tradition of rural and suburban communities who have mobilised to resist infrastructural projects by the state or corporate actors, ranging from campaigns against nuclear power and toxic industries in the 1980s through to 'anti-roads' campaigns against motorways in the 1990s (Leonard, 2006, 2008a, 2008b). This mobilisation, by the 'Shell to Sea' campaign against the Corrib Gas pipeline operated by corporate multinationals, throws up a number of questions about risk society, ecological modernisation, state policy and community movement responses to all of these issues, which will be interrogated in this chapter.

THEORETICAL FRAMEWORK

The theoretical framework for this chapter will include the perspectives of Critical Criminology and Rural Criminology. Critical Criminology provides a critique based on the political economy of a rural community which opposed corporate and state entities during the gas pipeline dispute. It also allows for a critique of the oppressive manner in which the Irish criminal justice system was used against the community protest group which emerged in resistance to the pipeline and development. Rural Criminology provides scope for a rural perspective on this dispute, based on the potential for the degradation of a rural community and its environment due to the pipeline and installation development. The rural community in County Mayo has fought for recognition of community rights since the Land League agitation of the late 1800s, and many involved in the gas pipeline dispute feel they are continuing in a local tradition of community rights advocacy.

As the local community is an indigenous 'Gaeltacht' or traditional Irish-speaking area, it has indigenous origins which have set it apart from those who have tried to impose perceived injustices such as mass evictions, removal of farming and fishing rights and industrial development by the state under British or Irish rule, or corporate entities. I argue that this form of rural response as having its origins in a type of 'rural sentiment' (Leonard, 2008a, 2008b). The study will utilise 'Resource curse theory' (Aughty, 1993) to demonstrate the inability of a post-colonial country such as Ireland to utilise its resources without the intervention of corporate multinationals, who don't have local interests at heart. The chapter will also use social movement framing theory to indicate how the protesters were able to extend their risk frame by increasing the sense of shared grievance surrounding local identity, sense of place and sense of exploitation by the corporate multinationals involved in the development of the gas pipeline.

A POLITICAL ECONOMY OF RESOURCE EXPLOITATION

The political economy of resource exploitation in this case involves the Irish state, who sold off their nation's resources for one of the lowest royalties ever negotiated with the multinational corporate sector. Over time, a number of Tribunals of Inquiry have been established to investigate the political class in Ireland over recent decades (Leonard, 2014). From both the critical and rural criminology perspective, the actions of the Irish state in establishing 'sweetheart deals' with corporate entities create problematic themes, such as rural resource exploitation and the use of national criminal justice systems to uphold these deals against the interest of the local communities involved.

According to Ruggiero and South:

> Power misused or used for profit to the exclusion of all else is likely to cause harm. Business and government interests exploit both environmental resources and human labour. But even more damaging is that, although all this may apply to market economies in general, hegemonic discourses around 'growth and freedom' have, during the last few decades, intensified the potential destructiveness of enterprise. In this respect, neo-liberal doctrines contradict their very axioms: namely, that the full costs of transactions must be borne by the involved parties. (Ruggiero & South, 2013)

Successive Irish governments have had allegations of corruption against them, and there were many concerns voiced about the nature of the deals done between the state and multinational corporations in relation to off-shore resource exploration (Leonard, 2006, 2008a, 2008b, 2014). In the case of the gas resources off the Irish coast, the deals signed off by the state provided royalties lower than many developing nations received for their oil or gas, with the gas only being piped to major cities. Many locals were as concerned about the nature of the deal being entered into by their government as they were about local community and environmental issues caused by the pipeline. Carrington and Perira (2011) in their study of similar conflicts in Australia argue that this type of dispute between a concerned community and both state and corporate agencies can be seen as a social justice issue. Szasz (1998) has termed this form of environmental justice dispute as 'ecopopulist', where campaigns can extend their movement framing beyond their backyardist or 'NIMBY' (Not In My Backyard) origins, by establishing a wider protest framework which incorporates social and political concerns.

This analysis of social or environmental justice campaigns includes forms of case study methods such as the 'exploratory', 'explanatory' and descriptive' (Yin, 2008). Exploratory case studies provide holistic examinations of the background to salient cases of environmental justice such as that of the 'Shell to Sea' campaign. With explanatory case studies providing an understanding of the significant criteria surrounding environmental or social justice's process and mobilisations, observations are then combined with the gathering of documentary evidence to provide a deeper understanding of critical and rural criminology in theory and in practice.

CASE STUDY

In Ireland, the first years of this century were characterised by a period of rapid development and large-scale infrastructural projects. One such development was located in County Mayo in the west of Ireland. In 2001, multinationals with state contracts planned to construct a gas pipeline from the Corrib Field, which lay 100 miles off-shore, and onshore across the farmlands of the area. Planning permission was also acquired for a processing-plant on a 400-acre site near local farmland. In 2002, an amendment to state law allowed commercial industries access to private lands with a Compulsory Acquisition Order (CPO). A CPO was issued for land on the planned route of the pipe – over the objection of the owners; and five of these farmers ('The Rossport Five') were eventually to spend 94 days in prison in 2005. The projected pipeline, which was planned to run alongside the homes of the farming families, was seen as a dangerous hazard to homes and the community nearby. The load of such a pipeline would be carried at a pressure five times greater than that allowed in Irish domestic gas pipes. The local community would derive no economic benefit, since the gas was to be pumped to larger cities like Galway and Dublin. The response from the local framing community was one of opposition to the pipeline and plant. The motivations of rural protestors run deep. Their 'Shell to Sea' campaign originated from a primordial concern for their local hinterlands. Green philosophical responses are more likely to be found emerging from the indigenous subconsciousness of native populations such as those in rural areas as part of a community's subliminal relationship with its surroundings. For the rural protestors, their lives and the land reclaimed from the sea by their forbears are as one, forging a relationship that is as 'green' as it gets. While academics, industrialists and the state present themselves as environmentalists, it is the native wisdom of the rural community in Mayo which can be seen as truly eco-centric, due to their primary concern for 'The Land'.

From a critical criminology viewpoint, there is some degree of oppression in this case. The landowners had been summoned to the Irish High Court on four separate occasions at great personal cost. The High Court Action taken against the residents restrained the named defendants from refusing to allow pipe-laying on their lands. They had sought evidence of the CAOs before they would allow entry to their lands. This evidence was held back for up to two and a half years. A further attempt to gain entry to the lands at the site was followed by the summoning of five local men to the High Court. The men were all charged with breaching the interim order of the court after the men confirmed that they could not abide by the terms of the Court Order. In a statement to the court one defendant summed up the men's position:

> The farms form the basis of the identity of the people. Monetary compensation cannot compensate for undermining the social identity of the people. (Leonard, 2007)

The five farmers were jailed for contempt of court, despite one of the defendants stating from his prison cell that Articles 40 and 43 of the Irish Constitution demand that the State protect the fundamental rights and property of every citizen. With their incarceration, the local men would become the news story of the summer of 2005. The national press held daily updates of the campaign and the men and their family's acquired celebrity status. As they were taken away to prison local supporters surrounded the men's land to prevent the corporate group from gaining access. The campaign took on a new momentum as trade unionists, anti-globalisation activists and environmentalists began to support the campaign.

The campaign received widespread support. One example of this was from a west of Ireland parliamentarian who would go on to become President of Ireland. Michael D. Higgins of the Labour Party supported the 'Shell to Sea' campaign at a rally in Galway in 2005, stating:

> There is now an absence of moral courage well the people of the left said that our resources shouldn't be taken from us. These five men in jail are a reflection on law and morality because they wanted to protect their families. The injunction is flawed because the state hadn't given permission for the pipeline. These men have contempt for an injunction that is based on a lie. (Micheal D. Higgins, Labour Party President and current Irish President, 2005, Leonard, 2006)

Higgins makes references to 'moral courage' in his speech, framing the campaign as a contest about social morality and the collective conscience that had been breached by the corporate entity's aggressive response to local resistance. In a Durkheiman way, Higgins was connecting this issue and with the collective moral conscience, inviting others to join the protest as it violated their moral rights and was built around a moral frame. The English television station Channel 4 ran a news item which questioned the plans for an onshore pipeline and terminal in Rossport. The report claimed that locals had faced pressure to sign over their property and that the deal with the Royal Dutch Shell company was 'unprecedented in Europe' (*The Irish Examiner*, November 27, 2002).

Records were produced in the report which raised allegations of political interference and pressure being brought to bear on the local County Council's planning committee while it was also revealed that the then ruling Irish political party *Fianna Fáil* received donations from two of the companies involved in the Corrib Field operation. The Channel 4 report was critical of the manner in which Ireland's national resources were being given away without any revenue making its way back to the Irish taxpayer, with the Corrib deal giving a poorer return than similar deals signed in Nigeria (Leonard, 2008a, 2008b). That autumn, the connection between Ireland and Nigeria was strengthened by the appearance of Dr. Owens Wiwa, brother of the murdered author and anti-oil industry activist Ken Saro Wiwa, who backed the campaign against Shell when he visited Ireland. The campaign now had a transnational context, stretching from Norway to Nigeria. 2005 also saw the release of a report on the Corrib gas issue by the Centre for Public Inquiry (CPI). The report claimed that the National Planning Board was subjected to 'external pressure' on the issue, a claim the Board denied (Leonard, 2006). The report's executive summary put forward a number of findings. This included criticism of the state's handling of resources and royalties, its regulatory framework surrounding the introduction of the Compulsory Acquisition Orders (CAOs) and the gas pipeline, the location of the pipeline and terminal and the supervision of work carried out at the site. The report was also critical of the access provided for Shell executives to senior politicians, including the Taoiseach (Connolly & Lynch, 2005). The Corrib pipeline was irregular 'due to its operational pressure, lack of historical data in the system evaluation, proximity to people and dwellings and deficiencies in the demonstration of maximum pipeline pressure' (Kuprewicz, 2005, p. 6).

While campaigners welcomed the CPI report, the subsequent politically motivated closure of the Centre threw a cloud over its findings, further demonstrating the degree of complexity and political intrigue which surrounded this issue. Throughout the winter of 2007 a series of clashes between police and protestors who wanted to prevent further work on the pipeline and terminal at Erris made national news. However this once localised campaign had caught the imagination of the Irish public and those activists beyond who felt a common sense of moral violation by the bullying tactics of Shell and Statoil, with networks extending from Norway to Nigeria. The campaign continues to gain support, and the 'Shell to Sea' campaign was awarded the Goldman environmental prize in recognition of the effectiveness of their campaign. The twists and turns of this dispute have challenged the thinking of those involved, while shaping the wider understandings of the issues involved. Ultimately, the success of 'Shell to Sea's' protest has been its impact in changing the cultural discourse of a changing Ireland comes to embrace the concerns of this small West of Ireland community (Leonard, 2008a, 2008b).

The Irish Department of Justice requested that Atlantic Philanthropies, which funded the Centre for Public Inquiry, cease it support for that organisation, with the Centre closing as a result. This form of political involvement again raised issues about the moral framework surrounding the Corrib Gas pipeline issue, from a critical criminology perspective.

The main framing strategies of the 'Shell to Sea' campaign emerged around this combination of local populism and a wider expression of cultural nationalism alongside traditional campaign focus points such as health and safety concerns:

- The dangers and risk posed by the pipeline.
- Local duty to defend families and property.
- The unsavoury behaviour of the multinational and the state.
- The misrepresentation of facts on the issue.
- The prioritisation of corporate profits over local concerns (Leonard, 2008a, 2008b).

Taking a rural criminology perspective, the risk frame highlighted the dangers posed by the onshore gas pipeline which was planned to run alongside the homes of many families in the area. The then Minister of State confirmed in a written reply in the Irish parliament to concerned deputies that such a pipeline would be unparalleled in Ireland, Europe or elsewhere. The rated pressure of the pipeline would exceed that used by The Irish Gas Authority nearly five times while the gas that would be transported through the pipeline with unrefined oil and water could cause blockages and be risk-prone with obstructions occurring far from the gas field where they could be treated. A further concern raised by the campaigners was the lack of any material benefit for the local community that was bearing the brunt of these risks as all of the gas would be piped through the county into larger cities such as in Ireland. In this way, the campaigners were able to extend their risk frame by increasing the sense of shared grievance surrounding local identity, sense of place and sense of exploitation which was running high throughout the county. For the campaigners this approach would have the double negative effect of having all profits repatriated to the multinationals while the chance to develop the west's gas supply would also be lost to the country's sprawling urban area.

The multinational attempted to serve their state-backed Compulsory Acquisition Orders (CAOs) on locals in the area in January 2005. By March the company had applied to the High Court for restraining orders against local landowners, the five men and some of their neighbours. Subsequently Shell began excavating peat from the proposed refinery site. Locals were unable to get past heavy machinery on the one narrow road into the area. As the multinationals planned for 70 truck movements a day during construction confrontations became inevitable. Local residents turned for help to sympathetic local politicians, who claimed that the 'people who have been compelled to have the Corrib gas upstream pipeline adjacent to their homes are scared out of their minds' (Connolly & Lynch, 2005, p. 43).

From a critical criminology perspective, the justice system's response was oppressive. The Irish High Court Action taken against the residents restrained the named defendants from refusing to allow pipe-laying on their lands. The landowners had been summoned to the High Court on four separate occasions at great personal cost. The landowners had sought evidence of the CAOs in due course before they would allow entry to their lands. This evidence was held back for up to two and a half years. A further attempt to gain entry to the lands was followed by the summoning of five local men to the Irish High Court. These local men were all charged with breaching the interim order of the court after the men confirmed to the court that they could not abide by the terms of the Court Order (Connolly & Lynch, 2005, p. 45).

The five local men were jailed for contempt of court despite, as one of the defendants would state from prison, the fact that the constitution under Articles 40 and 43 demand that the State protect the fundamental rights and property of every citizen. With their incarceration the 'Rossport 5' would become a national and international news story. Many national and local newspapers held daily updates of the campaign and the men and their families took on celebrity status. As the men were taken away to prison local supporters surrounded the men's land to prevent workmen from gaining access. The campaign took on a new momentum.

The imprisoning of these farmers hanged the minds of many locals who had previously favoured the terminal. The protest campaign began to mobilise on a wider level as picketing, rallies and rallies were extensively stepped up. The significant alliances which the families had forged took up the campaign as key figures from local trade unions, politics and colleges organised the committee. Another mobilisation strategy of the campaign following the men's imprisonment was the placing of pickets on service stations around the country. In addition, a series of rallies were held nationwide that drew thousands of ordinary people who wished to express their concern about the imprisoning of the five men. Terminals were also the target of organised blockades by environmentally minded 'ecowarriors', while ecological societies from the University sector were also prominent at many of the campaign's events. A 'Solidarity camp' was established as a campsite vigil by these groupings. The camp is still active. The wider support base gave rise to a mobilisation of support unparalleled in previous environmental campaigns. Support for campaign came from all levels of

Irish society including local political groups, trade unions and the anti-globalisation network, as well as artists and musicians.

This cross section of support allowed 'Shell to Sea' to extend their framing process to incorporate a much wider remit as oppositional politics and cultural discourse were embraced. This is a strategy or object which environmental campaigners had attempted to create over the various campaigns of the last four decades (Leonard, 2008a, 2008b). The fulcrum of this evolution was, undoubtedly, the imprisonment of the five men. However, while similar fates have been meted out to protestors in recent years it must be said that the men's eloquent statements in defense of their actions during their months in prison won a great deal of public support for their cause. Even though the men were fully committed to their cause they were shocked at their treatment claiming that they were only seeking justice:

> We were put in prison for protecting ourselves. They said we broke the law but we only broke an injunction that shouldn't have been there. We never did any harm. We were just trying to protect our families and rather than listen to us they put us into prison for 94 days. (Leonard, 2008a, 2008b).

While the camp continued to attract sympathisers and grassroots activists and students from around the country and abroad the protests continued with events occurring at an almost daily rate. A 'National Day of Protest' was called against the corporates involved. Organised pickets occurred at stations across Ireland. A national petition was also organised as thousands put their signature or e-mailed in messages of support to the 'Shell to Sea' website (http://www.shelltosea.org). Their webpage provided the campaign with a powerful tool in the highly computer-literate Ireland. Grassroots bloggers and activist websites gave prominence to the campaign and links between protestors across the globe were established via the internet. It could be said that this new communication technology provided the links to environmental circuits which existed nationally and globally. Internet technologies opened up possibilities for environmental campaigners that also facilitated their ability, not just to gain media coverage but to shape the news and influence the public perception of the debate. Such power is unwieldy unless applied well and 'Shell to Sea' ran a compelling campaign. The campaigner's website was a mobilising resource in itself providing updates and messages. Moreover, it set out a series of strategies which activists would support, such as suggesting participation through:

- Inviting activists to the Solidarity Camp to learn more about the issue.
- Supporting the campaign's all-Ireland speaking tour
- Financial donation and Fundraising (Leonard, 2008a, 2008b).

The provision of this array of campaign strategies on the campaign site allowed the campaign to circumvent established media outlets and provided the widest range of involvement for the public from petition signing to the organisation of blockades. By mobilising in this extensive manner the campaign became a resource in itself as the centrepiece to a burgeoning grassroots eco-movement which encompassed locals, environmentalists, students and political activists in a manner not witnessed since Ireland's anti-nuclear protests in the early 1980s (Leonard, 2008a, 2008b).

One response from the state to the controversy was the announcement of a safety review of the Corrib gas pipeline by the Irish government. The relevant department stated that officials had inspected the onshore site and that in his opinion a serious breach of the consents given to the corporates had occurred. In the hope of resolving the dispute government officials ordered the dismantling of the length of gas pipeline that had already been assembled at the site. The petroleum company announced that it would lay off 128 workers at the site if the protest continued (Leonard, 2008a, 2008b). The state's initiative included the establishment of a technical group to monitor the Corrib gas project which included senior civil servants, geographers, engineers and legal experts (Leonard, 2008a, 2008b). As the men completed their first month in prison, Shell were coming under increased pressure to lift their injunction to allow the men to go free, particularly in the wake of the breach of its technical consents. Legal attempts were made to free the men due to the fact that Ministerial consent had been given for preparatory work only, rather than the construction and installation at the site. Opposition leaders also called for the men's release. 'Shell to Sea' spokespersons cautiously welcomed the Minister's intervention although the campaign noted the timing of the announcement on the eve of a major rally in support of the men and in the week of their latest court hearing. A National Rally in Dublin attracted over 2000 people. Pickets were arranged in diverse locations such as the Norwegian embassy in Brussels and at political events. Over 1000 people picketed outside Shell petrol stations that month (Leonard, 2006).

Further criticism of the state's policies was highlighted in a local news feature on the issue by an American energy regulator. All concerned parties including the protestors, industry and the political sector were constrained by the lack of 'uniform safety requirements for gas pipelines', a policy which was 'at odds with international practice' (Leonard, 2007). The article contrasted safety regulators in the United States for gas pipelines that emanated from two government agencies including an Office of Pipeline Safety with what was called 'a frightening lapse' in the regulatory framework. Pipelines in the United States are also protected by a 'certificate of public convenience and necessity' (Leonard, 2007), words which would have a ring of irony to the imprisoned farmers. Public enquiries and written submissions were an integral part of the licensing system in the United States. As the men spent their 50th day in jail they must have found such regulatory discrepancies to be very questionable. While the petroleum companies negotiated with the local county council on the issue the men offered to engage in dialogue with representatives of the corporate multinationals if the Court injunction against them was lifted.

Executives from the multinationals claimed the injunction was a matter for the courts but welcomed the men's statement nonetheless. The multinational claimed it would be open to legal challenges if it relinquished the injunction, something which was rejected by many. One strategic response of the men in prison was their claim that the refusal to lift the injunction was preventing them from preparing their case for the full hearing on the issue and that as the industry had suspended work on the site the injunction now made no sense. The men accused of petroleum companies of not being interested in dialogue and said that they were obliged to defend their families as the state had refused to do so. According to the protestors, the industries involved 'were more interested in their strategy than the law' (Leonard, 2008a, 2008b). The protestors accused the multinationals of 'vindictiveness' for not withdrawing the injunction claiming that they could not impede work at the site while it was non-operational. Community groups called for the injunction to be released while the Irish Labour Party stated that the continued imprisonment of the men was 'bordering on becoming a national disgrace' (Leonard, 2008a, 2008b).

In September 2005 the Irish High Court President freed the imprisoned farmers. The court stated that the injunction 'no longer served any useful purpose'. The farmer's legal council asked the court to also remove the order of committal claiming it to be 'coercive' and that the men should not face further sanction in the future. However, while the men offered an apology for breaking the court order they refused to give an undertaking on any future activities. In a further development, the High Court indicated to all representatives of the multinationals that he wanted these companies to address its breach of the Minister's licenses but that he would not deal with that issue while the men languished in prison (Leonard, 2006).

As the men walked free with their jubilant supporters they vowed that their campaign would go on. The issue was set to continue the following month as Shell stated its intention to pursue the matter of a permanent injunction against the Rossport 5 and any other objectors to the pipeline. The safety review established by the state was also scheduled for that month. The state announced plans to appoint a mediator to negotiate with both parties. As they returned to Mayo traditional bonfires lit the way along their route back to their homes. According to the farmers, their campaign showed that 'Irish people expect a higher state of democracy and they expect more of their Government in relation to people's safety and welfare' (Leonard, 2008a, 2008b). The farmers also indicated their willingness to return to prison if necessary. Prominent campaign supporters indicated that the extension of the campaign into Norway during their general election had played a significant part in building the momentum that led to the men's release. The newly elected administration was believed to have instigated the meeting between senior Statoil executives and the Irish government the week before the men's release in the wake of the visit of protestors to Norway. The protestors said that this meeting with Statoil and the Norwegian authorities revealed that 'they did not know what was happening and were shocked by it' (Leonard, 2008a, 2008b). It was felt that the men would have remained in prison but for his Norwegian trip and subsequent intervention. Campaign supporters had met to work out the best way to get the men released. As the Norwegian government owned 71% of Statoil it was decided to bring the campaign to Oslo, extending the geographical bounds of the campaign further.

Protestors were able to plan the trip with the help of Norwegian journalists and trade unionists whom the group had developed links with during the campaign. They supplied the campaign with valuable details, contacts and lists of who to meet during their time in Oslo, maximising the impact of their mission. They were able to get national exposure on Norwegian television as a result at a time when Dublin City Council were threatening to prosecute anyone who put up posters advertising the campaign's Dublin rally. The most significant meetings during their trip were with Norwegian Oil and Energy Minister and senior industry managers who would meet with Irish government representatives a week after the campaigns mission (Leonard, 2008a, 2008b). While the men celebrated with families and supporters they continued to plan the next phase of their campaign. They insisted that the Irish government should participate in any talks between the families and Shell claiming that 'the state cannot remain neutral in this'. The men thanked the public who had supported them while they were in prison. The men won further support from the public for their eloquence and resolve on their release including the manner in which they highlighted conditions facing the inner-city youth who were their prison mates in prison. The men claimed they got no special treatment in the prison but were well treated by their fellow prisoners.

CONCLUSION

While this dispute was initially about an onshore pipeline being located near a number of local homes and farms, it has long since moved away from that single issue and has come to represent a range of social and political concerns and about the corporate power of resource extraction companies and the asymmetrical relationships with land holders to compel their compliance and deference. While many in the area have fears about the imposition of the pipeline this fear does not always extend to a full understanding of whether the pipeline is safe or not, nor what economic benefits it may or may not bring. According to the campaign many locals 'simply do not want it'. The pipeline represents an unwelcome intrusion into their land and community. It is this very sense of place that the campaigners wish to protect and the threat posed by outsiders has reawakened a determined resistance in the local community that has its roots in an identity born of the past with little concern for notions of 'progress'. Ironically, the Irish government would have been keen to repeat the economic growth of both the host nations of the corporate groups involved, in both the Netherlands (Shell) and Norway (Statoil). Both nations displayed 'Resource curse' theory issues (Aughty, 1993), such as 'the Norwegian Paradox' and the 'Dutch Disease', both of which demonstrate the varying outcomes faced by small to medium countries which develop their economic resources. In the context of the globalised world, there are many pros and cons from resource development. Ireland stands to gain almost no royalties for the disruptive gas facility, except for a few hundred local jobs during its development.

A moral framework that values family and community over economic growth was a key frame of the campaign. This form of moral framing has a subconscious element to it which has been instinctively unleashed in many Irish disputes over time. A subsequent sacrifice to defend the blood lines rooted in the hinterlands has been witnessed over many centuries in Irish history, and has become a primary aspect in the development of *rural community sentiment* (Leonard, 2008a, 2008b). From a critical criminology perspective, the farmers' near 100 days in prison and the traumatic effect this injustice had on family and neighbours can be seen as a heavy handed response by the Irish justice system to the concerns of a local community. This trenchant stance has been acknowledged by the multinationals who have appointed local spokespersons to try and comprehend the depth of feeling directed against them. Alternative routes for the pipeline have been suggested to try to meet peoples' concerns. The dispute continued to gain headlines as protestors and police clashed at the site in recent years, with allegations of police abuse of protestors making headline news. The campaign was recognised as the protestors were awarded the international Goldman Environmental prize. The award was a timely acknowledgement of the efforts of the campaigners in the protection of their local community and environment, and establishes the case within the frameworks set out by White (2013) as an environmental justice issue and (Carrington & Perira, 2011) as a rights and social justice issue. The pipeline case also displays elements of the 'geographies of crime' set out by Carrington, McIntosh, and Scott (2010) in their study of mining disputes.

The protest campaign highlights the complex issue of a community response to an infrastructural project based on both a sense of grievance about the intrusion of the project in the area and fears about the safety of the gas pipeline. The response of the local community has emerged from a historically derived sense of place which has been articulated as part of a wider discursive framing process that links cultural nationalism with community-based environmentalism. Politically the issue can be traced back to the long-standing state policy of selling off resources while facilitating land acquisitions by partners. Local political response has been mixed with some supporting the 'campaign while mainstream councillors and national representatives were ambivalent or chose to favour on-shore development' (Leonard, 2008a, 2008b).

The shift in policy direction undertaken by successive neo-liberal Irish governments led to a move towards a primarily ecological modernisation-orientated policy framework (as set out by the European Union). The emphasis on economic growth over environmental protection or concerns for communities has subsequently become a priority. This has been exacerbated by the Eurozone crisis and bailout of the Irish economy by the International Monetary Fund (IMF) since 2008 (Leonard & Botetzagias, 2011). Ultimately, the costs of economic growth have led to greater environmental degradation and an undermining of significant aspects of the nation's heritage. In particular, rural communities have borne the cost of Ireland's transition from a rural agrarian society into an industrialised and globalised economy, leading to the Corrib Gas dispute reflecting elements of 'resource curse' theory. While communities have demonstrated a commitment to retaining some aspect of the traditional values and heritage of the 'Emerald Isle', the state's policy of prioritising rapid infrastructural development in order to underpin private consumption and multinational investment over local community services may prove to be ill advised as fluctuations on the global markets continue. As the cycle of the 'Celtic Tiger' gave way to the era of IMF sponsored austerity in the wake of the post-2008 economic crisis, the ecological values and concerns of these local communities may provide a new direction for the post economic boom austerity era.

REFERENCES

Aughty, R. (1993). *Sustaining development in mineral economies: The resource curse thesis*. London: Routledge.

Carrington, K., McIntosh, A., & Scott, J. (2010). Globalization, frontier masculinities and violence: Booze, blokes and brawls. *British Journal of Criminology*, *50*(3), 393–413.

Carrington, K., & Perira, M. (2011). Assessing the social impacts of the resources boom on rural communities. *Rural Society*, *21*(1), 2–20.

Connolly, F., & Lynch, R. (2005). *The great Corrib gas controversy*. Dublin: Center for Public Inquiry.

Kuprewicz, R. (2005). *The proposed Corrib onshore system an independent analysis*. Dublin: Centre for Public Inquiry.

Leonard, L. (2006). *Green nation: The Irish environmental movement from Carnsore Point to the Rossport 5*. In Ecopolitics Series (Vol. 2). Galway: Greenhouse Press. Drogheda: Choice Publishing.

Leonard, L. (2007). The moral framing of a resource dispute. *Studies: Irish Quarterly Review, Winter*, *16*(4), 463–483.

Leonard, L. (2008a). *Rapid development & community mobilization in the Republic of Ireland*. Community Development, 07/2008.

Leonard, L. (2008b). *The environmental movement in Ireland*. Dordrecht: Springer. doi:10.1007/978-1-4020-6812-6

Leonard, L. (2014, May). Cultural criminology, governmentality and the liquidity of the failing state: The view from Ireland. *Critical Criminology*, *22*(2), 293–306.

Leonard, L., & Botetzagias, I. (Eds.). (2011). Sustainable politics and the crisis of the peripheries: Ireland and Greece. In *Advances in ecopolitics* (Vol. 8). Bingley: Emerald.

Ruggiero, V., & South, N. (2013). Toxic state–Corporate crimes, neo-liberalism and green criminology: The hazards and legacies of the oil, chemical and mineral industries. *International Journal for Criminal Justice and Social Democracy*, *2*(2), 12–26.

Shell to Sea. Reetrieved from http://shelltosea.com, http://corribsos.com. Accessed in 2005 and 2014.

Szasz, A. (1998). *Ecopopulism: Toxic waste and the movement for environmental justice*. Minneapolis, MN: University of Minnesota Press.

White, R. (2013). Resource extraction leaves something behind: Environmental justice and mining. *International Journal for Crime and Justice*, *2*(2), 21–26.

White, R. (2014). Land theft as rural eco-crime. *International Journal of Rural Criminology*, *1*(2), (November 2012).

Yin, R. (2008). *Case study research: Design and methods*. Thousand Oaks, CA: Sage.

CHAPTER 6

ENERGY☆

ABSTRACT

The 2016 announcement of plans for a large new UK nuclear plant at Hinkley Point, just 250 miles from Ireland's coast, was met with concern by many Irish people. Paradoxically, nuclear power was rejected in Ireland in 1979 with the development of the coal burning plant at Moneypoint in County Clare, and outlawed as an energy option in 1999, yet the country still utilises electricity from the UK's power grid, which includes energy derived from nuclear power. Ireland's interconnected energy grid includes Northern Ireland and the Republic. This chapter will examine the issues surrounding Ireland's energy policy. In particular, it will focus on the debates that have occurred in Ireland in relation to the use of nuclear energy.

Keywords: Nuclear power; energy; protest; festival; Green; techno-centric

INTRODUCTION

While traditionally the political Left has pinpointed control of the means of production as the crucial issue of political contestation, environmental politics is more concerned with how the means of production impact upon the environment and to what extent this is acceptable in society. Nonetheless, mainstream political structures have continued to concentrate on the development of society which threatens the environment. Environmentalists have responded to this by addressing the technical nature of industrial development, and the need to critique that development through deep green politics, or alternatively, to try to compromise and regulate industry. A difference has been detected in both aspects of environmental thought in so far as perspectives vary as to whether industrial development should be slowed down, through eco-modernist principles such as 'BATNEEC' or 'the best available technology not entailing

☆Some of this article was originally published in Leonard (2009).

excessive costs' or 'The polluter pays principle', or whether industrial growth should be reversed and replaced with a more eco-centric social planning. Pepper (1993) and O'Riordan (1981) have defined such environmental diversions as that of a 'technocentric perspective as opposed to an eco-centric' view:

- Techno-centrism recognises environmental problems but believes our current form of society will always solve them and achieve unlimited growth ('the cornucopian view') or more cautiously that by careful economic and environmental management they can be negotiated ('the accommodators').
- Eco-centrism views humankind as part of a global eco-system and subject to ecological laws. These … constrain human action, particularly through imposing limits to economic population growth (Pepper, 1993, pp. 33–93).

In other words, the root of techno-centrism lies in social and political compromise between the earth's resources and human development with technology as the cutting edge of this manipulation of the earth's resources. Techno-centric approaches are determined with no overhaul of human social systems envisaged and despite recognition of the inherent ecological problems of this analysis. Eco-centrism, conversely places humankind not to the fore of the global eco-system, but rather sees humanity as part of an organic whole, with a moral imperative to restrain activity and growth and to interact and co-operate with the greater eco-systems that populate the earth. This view holds a respect for a pristine, natural world in its own right before any aspect of human economy and development is considered with human beings living in a spirit of cooperation and ecumenism with the environment. The 'deep green' view of environmentalism had its roots in the ecological, feminist and other new social movements of the 1960s and 1970s and has challenged the hierarchical hegemony of political dominance and technological development over social and ecological systems across the globe. Deep green ideology goes beyond old left-wing attempts at 'controlling the means of production' or of deconstructing class systems and sets its point of origin before the era of revolution to the beginning of modernity and the age of Enlightenment. By questioning the concept of social order based on expansive development which had its roots in the Enlightenment project present day environmental protests have rejected the concept of a technologically driven modernity in itself, radically moving beyond the position of 'sustainable development' by questioning the validity of development from an eco-centric perspective. Bookchin spells out this premise with a view on these challenges of hierarchical systems of development:

> Ecology raises the issue that the very notion of man's dominance of nature stems from man's dominance of man. Feminism reaches even further and reveals that the domination of man by man actually originates in the domination of woman by man. Community movements implicitly assert that in order to replace social domination by self-management a new type of civic self … must be restored … to challenge the all-pervasive state apparatus. (Bookchin, 1980, p. 15)

RISK SOCIETY

Andrew Szasz examines the changing reactions to increased environmental problems in society, which he feels are symptomatic of 'a resigned, fatalistic environmentalism' (Szasz, 2007, p. 1). This analysis can be linked with the understanding of a poorly planned and toxic existence put forward by Beck in his portrayal of a 'Risk Society'. Essentially, this outlook views the earth in a hazardous light as rampant industrialisation pushes the planet to the brink of a catastrophe caused by a 'bewitchment of reason' (Beck, 1996) which holds that in the event of possible global calamity such as nuclear or chemical fallout prevailing attitudes are so transfixed by existing industrialised systems that no real provision has been made for such an event. Furthermore, it seems beyond the genius of current populations to envisage a system of human existence which, at least, doesn't threaten humankind and the planet we inhabit. Yet Beck sees no saviours in the environmental movement, which he claims is trapped in a naturalistic misunderstanding' (Beck, 1996, p. 7). He furthers this argument by claiming the ecological movement 'reacts to and acts upon a blend of nature and society that remains uncomprehended, in the name of a nature no longer extant' ... which is held up as 'a model for the reorganisation of an ecological society' (*ibid.*).

Criticisms of the environmental movement from industrialists are commonplace but Beck's analysis of an overriding confusion as to the positioning of the paradigms that intersect the bounds of society and environment point to the need for interrogation of the cultural and ideological backdrop to environmental politics. In doing so, this book addresses the varying strands of ecological discourses, by surveying the writers mentioned above, as well as undertaking to analyse recent theoretical conceptualisations in relation to the environment and post-modernity, as well as some of the more diverse examples of environmental consciousness. Beck claims that 'ecological protest is a matter, not of natural but of cultural fact; a phenomenon of cultural sensibility and of the attentiveness of institutions' (Beck, 1996, p. 49). This assertion has its basis in the argument which characterises environmental concern as a cultural rather than purely ecological expression. Essentially, the argument highlights the difficulty in explaining the inherent meanings underlying environmental discourses. Political protests, ecological or otherwise, invariably follow from cultural rather than ideological grievances. As western culture has industrialised so too has a new emphasis been placed on protecting an environment once seen as the very impediment of human aspirations for development (Leonard, 2008).

All political ideologies shared at their core a belief in the betterment of humanity through the taming of the ferocity of nature. This is what makes aspects of deep green environmentalism distinctive from the rest of the ideological spectrum. While acknowledging the Left's position on the failure of industrialised capitalism to include large sections of the global population in its wake, deep Ecologism goes beyond protesting this as unjust and inequitable and goes on to advocate an overall rejection of human development based on industrialised, technologically driven expansion in favour of cooperation with the still ferocious natural world.

However, theoretical conceptualisation of environmental modernisation which relates to sustainable development of industrial and political processes does not always fit into policy agendas at the EU or national government level. Tensions remain between environmental directives and some policy objectives of economic and structural growth. To achieve some semblance of ecological consciousness many industries hire PR spokespersons that use ecologically friendly language to mask their true intentions. Such rhetoric allows multinationals to sell themselves (and their products) on an environmentally friendly basis and allows a greater threat to the environment to be sold to an unsuspecting public. As a result it is often left to enquiring bodies such as protest groups to oppose multinationals. Many such groups and protestors are portrayed as unreasonable extremists by the public relations mechanism of multinationals. This type of posturing has blurred the definitions which underpin ecological politics. As a result environmental discourses have taken on the dialogue of metaphor and imagery, becoming a part of post-modern representations of the fragmented relations which concern humankind, nature and the building of social networks both globally and locally. As environmental definitions fragment and as the strategies and movements surrounding ecological politics diversify multifarious strands of 'green' political, cultural and social analysis vie with each other in an attempt to engage the public perception of what it is that 'environmental' actually means for them. These ecological discourses become central to the conceptualisations which define the environment. Furthermore, these definitions also challenge the discourses previously set by the parlance and paradigms of industrial society (*ibid.*).

Through this discursive contestation of social paradigms, ecological political debate has changed society's vision of itself as well as altering the dynamic of social and political relations, through protest and dialogue, since the last decades of the previous century. This questioning has enabled the growth of new approaches to many aspects of social and ecological relations and in turn has reshaped existing cultural and political discourses while also giving rise to new paradigms of distinct ecological expression. This new expression has come to be known as the green movement' or theoretically 'environmentalism'. If western thought contains elements of a dualistic anti-naturalism, then the theoretical conceptualisations stand aside from previous political aspirations in the Western sphere of influence, while fundamentally laying down a challenge to the social constructs which promote an ongoing form of accelerated development.

However, there are two variations of environmental theory which can be used to divide the various elements within ecological thought. One contends that the environment can be 'managed' in conjunction with industrial development. As such this viewpoint, which includes theories such as Ecological

Modernisation and Sustainable Development, is in conflict with the 'deep green' school of thought. The 'managerial approach' contends that 'environmental problems ... can be solved without fundamental changes in present values of patterns of production and consumption'. Theorists have argued that aspects of radical ecologism are disconnected from political reality, claiming that much of what passes for green politics is based on a form of 'anti-humanism' which lacks a rational basis (Bookchin, 1995). It can also be argued that green politics has provided a focus for the type of community-based protest movements that can address the democratic deficit created by over-bureaucratic and hierarchical administrations, at both the global and national level. By providing an outlet for social protest deep green environmental movements are addressing the onset of democratic deficit in society. In so doing, green politics has provided a basis for political movement rather than the type of entrenched ideological positions which have emanated from traditional left or right wing politics. In other words, the basis for green political protests may not necessarily be a strong belief in green politics. However, the types of protests which have become identified with the environmental movement have at their core not just ecological issues but also a representation of an understanding that the type of expansive capitalism which pits polluting industries against local communities in the name of jobs and profit. Moreover, a hegemonic response to the discord of public protest has been seen in what Dryzek (1997) has described as 'the Repertoire of Administrative Rationalism' which represents an institutional response to environmental issues. Dryzek describes aspects of this approach:

- Professional Resource-Management Bureaucracies: Consisting of 'natural resource management' policy making, usually in the areas of national parks, marine, sea and geophysic concerns.
- Pollution Control Agencies: The use of regulations and directives to control pollution.
- Regulatory Policy Instruments: The use of regulations and directives to control pollution.
- Environmental Impact Assessment: Administrative (and industrial) assessment of environmental damage.
- Expert Advisory Commissions: The use of scientific and technological expertise in relation to environmental issues at the behest of senior tiers of government.
- Rational Policy Analysis Technologies: The utilisation of the knowledge and methods of environmental science and engineering (Dryzek, 1997, pp. 64–70).

Such a response to environmental issues places an emphasis on science and technology and 'takes the structural status quo of liberal capitalism as given' (Dryzek, 1997, p. 74). Administrative Rationalism relies on a hierarchical approach and a regulatory response to environmental issues, within the existing bureaucratic and administrative structures of modern, capitalist societies. It assumes the 'subordination' of nature to development, people to state and experts and manager over communities. However, Administrative Rationalism, like the ecological modernisation discourse from which it emanated, is in a state of crisis as industrialised development impacts more and more on the environment. Weale described this administrative failing as an 'implementation deficit' (1992, pp. 17–18) which represents a deficit in the aims and actual achievements in relation to environmental matters at the administration level. We will look at three phases of movement resistance to energy projects in Ireland, nuclear in the late 1970s and early 1980s, incineration in the 1990s and 2000s and fracking in more recent years.

ANTI-NUCLEAR PROTESTS

As the crisis of peak oil looms, the debate about the viability of substituting fossil fuels with wind or wave energy has begun. One alternative which has been revived is nuclear power. Despite its radioactive waste, fears of meltdowns at plants or of terrorist attacks, a pro-nuclear lobby has raised the suggestion that nuclear power, currently declared illegal in the Republic of Ireland, could provide a part of the solution to the energy crisis. For instance, the Irish Green Party set out 'ten reasons' why nuclear power makes no sense for Ireland in their 2007 election manifesto. The 10 issues raised included prohibitive costs, renewable alternatives, nuclear not solving climate change, promotion of efficiency, lack of heat or transport options, the centralised nature of nuclear, radioactive waste, unsafe plants, depletion of uranium and links to nuclear weapons (Green Party, 2007). The extent of this opposition raises the question as to why the nuclear option is still on the agenda. Campaigns against nuclear power plants emerged from the concerns expressed by some US medical and science experts about the dangers of radiation exposure in the decades after the Second World War. While the horrors of Hiroshima and Nagasaki and fears of Cold War nuclear arms proliferation created a combination of grievance factors for many people, the global oil crisis of the 1970s had led to a renewed interest in nuclear energy as an alternative to fossil fuels. Many western nations such as the United States and Britain had developed their nuclear energy capacities, and as Ireland had little in the way of natural resources, some favoured the nuclear option as a potential policy for consideration. While many opposed nuclear power due to fears about the harmful effects of radiation, others saw it as a futuristic and efficient energy source (Leonard, 2008).

By the late 1960s and early 1970s the anti-war movement which had emerged around Vietnam War protests developed an interest in building up a resistance to nuclear power plants. Protests emerged in West Germany and France as activists, students and citizens came together to prevent nuclear plants from being constructed. Common cause was established between the anti-war protestors and environmentalists, while many feminists joined the anti-nukes campaign with the Greenham Common Women becoming synonymous with the movement in the United Kingdom by the 1980s. Anti-nuclear campaigns had already commenced in the United States where the site for one nuclear plant was occupied to prevent further construction. The nuclear accident at Three Mile Island proved to be a fundamental moment for both the industry and the anti-nuclear movement providing as it did a visible manifestation which seemed to validate the grievances of concerned activists. With its pacifist inception the anti-nuclear movement came to be characterised through its strategies of non-violent protest, occupation of nuclear power sites or military installations and the involvement of concerned students and women's groups. The emergence of the Campaign for Nuclear Disarmament (CND) came to replace the nuclear energy protests particularly in the aftermath of the Chernobyl disaster in 1986. This accident put grievances about nuclear power to the fore across the globe and certainly set nuclear energy back in the public's eye. Many states began to call for the phasing out of nuclear power in its wake (Kriesi et al., 1995, p. 151).

In recent years the Irish state, which tried to develop their own nuclear energy policy in the 1970s, began to challenge the UK government over the nuclear power plant at Sellafield, North Cumbria. In June 2005 the Irish government's legal team claimed that the discharge of nuclear waste into the Irish Sea was a breach of UN conventions. Despite the Irish state's poor record on environmental regulations the British government was taken to the European Court of Justice by their Irish counterparts but the case was rejected in January 2006. It was a far cry from the Carnsore protests in the late 1970s when the WISE 'nuclear power – no thanks' logo began to appear on the back windows of Volkswagen vans across the country. The debate about nuclear power has recently re-emerged in the wake of some environmentalists such as J. F. Lovelock proclaiming that nuclear power was still a viable and green alternative to the fossil fuels which have caused global warming.

BACKGROUND

The announcement by the All-Ireland Nuclear-Free Local Authorities Forum, which embraces councils from both sides of the border, calling for clarification on plans for a nuclear power station in Northern Ireland (*Irish Examiner*, 30 December 2005) rang a familiar, if somewhat alarming note with those who had opposed nuclear power in Ireland during the 1970s and 1980s. The campaign against the state's decision to build a nuclear power station in Carnsore Point, County Wexford in 1979 was the first large-scale instance of a collective response by environmentalists in Ireland. Many of the initial networks of the Irish eco movement were established as a result of the Carnsore campaign.

Links were established with environmentalists at home and abroad. The anti-nuclear issue would become an iconic one, characterised by an energetic alliance of many of the 'new left' social movements such as feminist, anti-war and student groups, as well as environmentalists who would go on to form the basis of the new social movements of the modern era.

A significant amount of popular opposition to nuclear power was mobilised through the Carnsore protests, creating the resource of a collective pool of environmental consciousness which future campaigns would draw upon. Perhaps more importantly, the state's plans for nuclear power were defeated by the Carnsore protestors, a victory which established a precedent which Irish environmentalists would aspire to, as policy was seen to be reversed through political protest. Plans for the use of nuclear power for the generation of electricity were first put forward in 1968. It was hoped that the nuclear option would help to meet projected increased demand for power in the 1970s. As the electric grid between the Electricity Supply Board, (ESB) and the Northern Ireland Electric Services (NIES) had been connected, the Irish state attempted to bring their policy of power generation in line with that of the United Kingdom, where the nuclear plant at Windscale, later Sellafield, had been in operation since 1951 (Leonard, 2008).

The fact that the Windscale plant had been involved in Britain's military nuclear project was one of the first issues picked up on by Irish anti-nuclear Protestors. Indeed, British and European anti-nuclear groups, who were primarily pacifists concerned about nuclear arms proliferation during the Cold War, provided important links with Irish anti-nuclear protestors. The state's project for nuclear power took a few different turns throughout the 1970s. Initial plans were put back in 1972, in favour of the development of the Kinsale gas field in County Cork (Dalby, 1998, p. 3). The onset of the global oil crisis in 1973 forced the state to again consider nuclear power as a possible option. As oil prices rose considerably as a result of oil shortages, a Nuclear Energy Board (NEB) was established to examine the feasibility of a nuclear power plant (*ibid.*). The planned location of this plant was Carnsore Point, a peninsula in County Wexford. In September 1974 the ESB applied to Wexford County Council for planning permission to build four energy stations, without specifying which technology was involved (*ibid.*).

Although all of the parties of government had examined options for nuclear power, the populist Fianna Fáil government led into power by Jack Lynch in 1977 became most associated with the Carnsore project. Under the supervision of the Minister for Industry, Commerce and Energy the momentum for a nuclear plant at Carnsore increased, while energy demands in the economically buoyant late 1970s grew. The brash 'men in mohair suits' who led Fianna Fáil at this time equated national growth and nation building with large-scale industrial projects. Historically, Fianna Fáil had promoted campaigns of self-sufficiency, characterised by the protectionism of the 1930s. Major projects such as the Ardnacrusha Hydro Electric Dam on the Shannon River or the industrial zone at Shannon airport were overseen by Fianna Fáil governments in an attempt to promote industrial infrastructure and economic growth. Carnsore nuclear plant was seen as a project which would bring Irish industry into the future.

This form of 'economic nationalism' (Baker, 1990, p. 50) was central to the political platform of Fianna Fáil, combining that party's inherent populism with a policy framework which would allow Ireland to grow beyond the economic constraints traditionally associated with dependency on the United Kingdom. The partitioning of Ireland into northern and southern states in 1922 had also shaped this post-colonial mindset as membership of the European Economic Community (EEC) in 1973 was seen as facilitating Ireland 'taking its place among the nations of the earth'. The development of an industrial sector in Ireland remained a key objective for successive governments. The Industrial Development Authority (IDA) was established in 1959 to encourage direct foreign investment by US multinationals in Ireland. Carnsore nuclear plant was seen as a vital component for presenting Ireland as a good destination for industrial investment. In many ways, the contestation of environmental disputes in Ireland can be placed in the context of the state's attempt to impose modernisation from above, through industrial and infrastructural projects and community resistance to such projects 'from below' in an attempt to retain traditional ways of life and autonomy from the state, particularly in rural communities (Leonard, 2008).

Seen in this context, the campaign against nuclear power at Carnsore Point can be seen in the fullest cultural context as part of an attempt to resist aspects of modernisation by a sceptical community. A number of objections to the application for planning permission for the Carnsore plant were received by Wexford County Council in 1972. There was also an initial wave of enthusiasm about the plant, led by local businesses. As early as July 1971, local groups including An Taisce, generations was questioned from the floor of this meeting (*ibid.*), indicating the degree of existing local concerns.

While all political parties supported the nuclear plant, local opposition on moral grounds was growing, reflecting the concepts of a finite and fragile 'planet earth' and concern for future generations represented during the first 'Earth Day' held globally since 1971. The NSA framed their objections to the plant on moral grounds, putting forward the following objections:

- A nuclear plant conflicted with high amenity area
- Cancer and leukaemia risks
- Disruption to local bird sanctuary (Lady's Island Lake)
- Radioactive waste as a national security risk
- Aggravation of fresh water consumption
- Long-term hazard of radiation in local eco-system
- Disruption to tourism

- No provision for domestic storage of radioactive waste if export proved impossible (Dalby, 1998, p. 7).

A further mobilisation tactic of the NSA was the collection of 2200 petitions against the plant, in February 1975, which had been presented to the local authority (*ibid.*). During 1974 potential supporters for a nascent anti-nuclear movement could be found in branches of Friends of the Earth which had opened in Dublin and Cork (Baker, 1990, p. 3). However, reduced demands for electricity due to economic recession in 1975 saw the plans for the plant put back again. By 1977 the recession had ended and Fianna Fáil was back in power. The Carnsore plant was back on the political agenda. This was reflected in the appointment of Professor C.T.C. Dillon from the Nuclear Energy Commission to become the chairman of the ESB in the spring of 1977. By that autumn the public inquiry at Windscale had revived local concerns about nuclear power.

The inquiry debated the nature of the future of Windscale as British Nuclear Fuel Ltd. (BNFL) attempted to make that plant the largest nuclear reprocessing plant, through its thermal oxide reprocessing plant (THORP) facility, in the wake of growing popular resistance to nuclear power in the United States. The subsequent protests became a unifying (2002, p. 416) force for the UK's anti-nuclear movement which would also benefit the Carnsore campaign.

The CONSERVE Committee produced a own document in July 1975 titled Legislation, Energy Conservation and the Balance of Payments which outlined the dangers and inefficiencies of nuclear power. The alternatives put forward in this document included better energy legislation, decentralised electricity stations and the co-generation of heat and power. The area of expertise was becoming more important for the anti-nuclear campaign, as academics such as Dr. Robert Blackith of Trinity College became more involved in the articulation of a critique of the nuclear issue. Dr. Blackith's book *The Power that Corrupts* was issued in 1976. This text included criticism of the ESB's approach to the nuclear issue in regard to providing the public with answers to these concerns (Dalby, 1998, p. 9). During 1977 the newly formed Friends of the Earth branch in Dublin continued the debate in a series of letters to the media. The national press featured articles on the subject of nuclear power, providing an outlet to those for and against the issue.

Another ally of the anti-nuclear campaign was John Carroll, president of Irish Transport and General Workers' Union (ITGWU). Carroll spoke at many anti-nuclear rallies, helped launch and would also edit a book with Petra Kelly of the German Greens who was doyen of the European environmentalists, called *A Nuclear Ireland?* (Baker, 1990, p. 55). The link between trades unions and the nuclear industry had been noted in the anti-nuclear World Anti-nuclear Service on Energy (WISE) newsletter in 1978. In their first edition, WISE, which developed the famous 'sun-smile' symbol with the 'nuclear power – no thanks' logo stated that workers were beginning to question their role in the 'energy – jobs link':

> They are beginning to realise that they are effectively terrorised by governments and energy monopolies with threats of mass unemployment unless atomic plants get built ... In some cases, links are starting to be established between the trades unions and the environmental and anti-nuke lobby ... to find out the real relationship of energy to jobs (*WISE Bulletin*, May 1978).

In the same issue, a list of trades unions sympathetic to the anti-nuke movement stated that the ITGWU was 'opposing the plans of the Irish government for giving Ireland its first atomic reactor' (*ibid.*) and included John Carroll's contact details.

As a result of increased networking by the various components of the Irish anti-nuclear movement, a wider consciousness developed around related issues such as Windscale's dumping of nuclear waste in the Irish Sea. The global campaign against nuclear armaments was also gaining strength and these issues increased interest in the anti-nuclear movement. Many people were concerned that the Carnsore plant could become involved in these processes in some way, particularly with groups such as Sovereignty Ireland (*ibid.*). Student groups such as the Student Christian Movement (SCM) continued to press the moral argument against nuclear power, with the support of 'new theology' Catholics and other Christian groups (Baker, 1998, p. 6). Another issue which came to light was the campaign against uranium mining in Donegal which involved direct action and the destruction of equipment (Baker, 1998, p. 9).

PROTESTS

By September 1978 a decision was made to occupy the land at Carnsore, with further plans for an anti-nuclear festival. A new group, based on the various elements of the anti-nuclear movement was formed for this purpose, called the Carnsore Collective (Baker, 1998, p. 10). At the same time Friends of the Earth began a national campaign encouraging people to lodge planning objections to the proposed site with Wexford County Council. These two tactics would form the main mobilisation strategy for the anti-nuclear campaigns with both the planning protest and the festival receiving prominent national and even international attention, with reports of the event featuring in the WISE Bulletin.

As anything up to between 7000 and 25,000 people descended upon Carnsore on the weekend of 18 August, the scale of the free festival was given front page coverage in the national press, with both the BBC and RTE featuring the protest. Special buses and trains brought the crowds to the site and a team of volunteers was on hand to provide stewarding, parking and crèche service (Dalby, 1998, p. 11). The festival was called 'Get to the Point', and featured a mixture of popular and folk musicians. In the crowd, radical left-wing and anarchist groups were well-represented. There were many tents which became forums for alternative politics, energy and lifestyles. Stalls sold books, newspapers and distributed leaflets and badges while most groups recruited new members at membership and information posts. By the end of the festival, it was suggested that over 7000 letters objecting to the nuclear plant had been lodged with Wexford council (Dalby, 1998, p. 12).

Following the festival the national press and opposition spokespersons such as Fine Gael's John Kelly began to call for an inquiry into the Carnsore Plant, something that was rejected by the Minister of State, Desmond O'Malley. By November the Minister had the support of the Confederation of Irish Industry which claimed nuclear power was 'essential for industrial development' (*ibid.*). Throughout the autumn of 1978, the anti-nuclear movement built on the momentum of the Carnsore festival, as events were held around the country. A major anti-nuclear meeting was held at the Mansion House in Dublin, while the ESB began to bulldoze the memorial cairn at Carnsore. One resource which was established was a newsletter for the combined anti-nuclear movement in Ireland. This was used to promote the 'Monster Meeting' held on 25 November in Dublin. In January, RTE broadcast a programme exclusively on the nuclear issue. This special edition of the popular 'Late Late Show' was hosted by Gay Byrne and featured speakers such as John Carroll and Petra Kelly. The programme was aired in the aftermath of a series of radio programmes on the issue. The show was a raucous affair, with the panel's statements being subject to interjections and booing from the audience. In between the lively debate, Christy Moore sang anti-nuclear ballads (Dalby, 1998, p. 14). The issue began to crystallise in the minds of the viewing public.

A NUCLEAR IRELAND?

In May 1978 an Energy Symposium was held under the auspices of the now defunct Irish Transport and General Workers Union (ITGWU) at the Royal Marine Hotel in Dun Laoghaire. Among the contributors to the Symposium were Dr. Blackith, Petra Kelly and Dr. Michael Flood, who was the Energy Consultant for Friends of the Earth (FOE) in London. The Unions were represented by John Carroll, the ITGWU's vice president, who chaired the symposium alongside union president Senator Fintan Kennedy and Dr. James Kavanagh, Auxiliary Bishop of Dublin. The State was represented by Minister Ray Burke. Submissions were divided into five sections. The first considered 'the Case for and against Nuclear Energy' with pro and anti-arguments being presented by Ray Burke and Dr. Blackith. John Carroll addressed the subject of 'Jobs and Nuclear Energy' while Petra Kelly discussed 'Nuclear Energy and the European Community'. 'Medical Considerations' were the subject of presentations by three medical doctors and paediatricians from the United Kingdom and the United States while the 'Ethical, Moral and Social Ramifications' of Nuclear Energy were debated by Sr. Bertell from New York

State University and Dr. Michael Flood of Friends of the Earth. The proceedings of this Conference were published under the title of A Nuclear Ireland? This text highlighted a number of the frames which the No Nukes campaign had already employed. The first of these was the moral frame.

Moral Frame

The preface to A Nuclear Ireland? opens with a poem from Karol Wojtyla, otherwise known as Pope John Paul II, whose iconic status was confirmed by the hundreds of thousands who flocked to see him on his visit to Ireland in 1978. The poem entitled 'The Armaments-Factory Worker' makes a connection between the sin of war and the participation of workers who build armaments. At the time the Cold War between the United States and the Soviet Union was at its zenith with thousands of nuclear missiles primed for catastrophic destruction if launched by either side. The use of Pope John Paul's poem on the need for conscious responsibility on everyone's behalf at a time when fears about possible nuclear war were heightened allowed the anti-nuclear campaign to grab the moral high ground.

This moral frame was underlined by the participation of the Auxiliary Bishop of Dublin, Dr. James Kavanagh, as well as through the submission of Sr. Rosalie Bertell, who had a Doctorate in Biostatistics, from New York. Sr. Bertell presented some of the ethical problems posed by nuclear proliferation in her contribution to the symposium. She claimed to have been politicised after being intimidated by a utility company after publishing her findings on links between nuclear power and leukaemia. Her findings demonstrated that the ageing process was advanced by 1 year for each rad exposure experienced, which was the equivalent of the yearly exposure for a worker in the US nuclear industry. This damage also causes increased susceptibility to leukaemia tumours and heart disease (Carroll & Kelly, 1980, p. 162). For Sr. Bertell these side-affects, which were more pronounced for at-risk groups such as infants or the elderly, posed a series of moral and ethical problems. These included the following issues:

- a shift from the father working to provide for his family to the father's exposure to radiation threatening his family including the unborn child;
- community exclusion from the nuclear industry's decision-making process on workers' health, community protection and family compensation;
- increased secrecy from industry and the state over nuclear power;
- the threat of nuclear pollution (*ibid.*).

Sr. Bertell made the moral point that a link between technology, jobs and health should coincide with increased civic participation and awareness. At the same time she called for increased controls over technology which should be employed for human good (*ibid.*). Sr. Bertell echoed the UN's call for sustainable development when she stated that a balanced approach was needed on energy.

The energy source we pursue cannot sacrifice the needs of future generations to satisfy the desires of present generations. The energy source we pursue cannot sacrifice truth-telling and concern for public health for economic good (Carroll & Kelly, 1980, p. 166).

The Health Risks Frame

The Health risks frame was presented by Dr. Helen Caldicott of Boston's Children's' Hospital. Originally from Australia, Dr. Caldicott had lobbied the French government about a decade before the sinking of the Greenpeace ship, the Rainbow Warrior, in New Zealand by French agents. In her submission Dr. Caldicott challenged a statement by Ray Burke that nuclear power would be 'good for the people'. Nuclear power 'had produced epidemics of leukaemia, cancer and genetic disease' (Carroll & Kelly, 1980, p. 106) according to Dr. Caldicott. She linked nuclear power with the armaments industry. The health risks of radiation were seen in instances of cancer and leukaemia in the United States, she claimed. The doctor also made reference to the threat of genetic engineering, a subject that would re-emerge in Ireland decades later. For Dr. Caldicott the damage caused by radiation to the human genetic system would have dreadful repercussions over generations. Another health risk raised by the doctor was the carcinogenic radioactive waste from nuclear power which remains toxic for half a million years (*ibid.*). Dr. Caldicott also predicted the dangers of terror groups stealing or obtaining materials for nuclear weapons.

The Economic Frame

The economic frame was put forward by the union chief, John Carroll. While he acknowledged the wider acceptance of the hazards of nuclear proliferation among the public Carroll wished to highlight the economic fallacy involved in the nuclear option. The 'doubtful economics', as he termed it, involved the development of energy plans that would leave Ireland's grid in the hands of the international cartels which controlled multinationals. In addition to the health risks highlighted by other speakers, Carroll argued that nuclear power plants were expensive due to the high security costs associated with similar projects elsewhere. The transportation of raw materials and nuclear waste was both expensive and hazardous in the extreme and would be subject to 'severe security measures' (Carroll & Kelly, 1980, p. 44). Furthermore, a nuclear plant at Carnsore would have been achieved at a high cost of over £300 million with US cases indicating rising costs for nuclear power plant construction and maintenance. Some American plants were unable to operate due to the scarcity of uranium supplies, which had rising costs of nearly 10% per annum. Another cost outlined by Carroll was the 'vast sums of money which the nuclear industry has spent on propagandising its wares' (*ibid.*).

Carroll was concerned that the high costs for building, maintaining and promoting a nuclear power plant would be taken from social services or other aspects of the state's development plans. Moreover, he anticipated only minor employment levels at the Carnsore plant with no extra employment that would have been achieved from a conventional power plant. At the same time resources for alternative energies such as wind and tidal power would be diverted to fund the nuclear plant which itself would struggle to reach full capacity due to 'shut downs and infrequency of operation that performance entails', with 'no guarantee that such a plant will operate during its lifetime at anything like an average 60% capacity which will add to the costs of the energy produced' (*ibid.*).

The European Frame

Petra Kelly outlined her vision for a better Europe which embraced 'a civic, non-violent community of various member states' (Carroll & Kelly, 1980, p. 89). For Kelly, a German of Irish extraction, Ireland at that point remained 'ecologically intact' (*ibid.*). Kelly outlined a cultural discourse which contextualised Ireland as a place of rural culture with an enduring 'loyalty to locality' (*ibid.*), which reflected a European ideal of traditional values. The shift to nuclear power would see Ireland become reliant on a centralised and erratic form of energy. The security threats surrounding nuclear power would affect Irish politics and society, leading to an over-emphasis on centralised technocratic power. The risks inherent in nuclear processing were so great that a controlled society would emerge in its wake, with implications for democratic freedom, according to Kelly. The results for Irish society were stark:

> The delicate web of social life called democracy will be torn and ripped apart due to the very nature of nuclear power and the monitoring and protection and surveillance necessary for the worker, the general population and the environment. (Carroll & Kelly, 1980, p. 91)

This combination of economic, cultural and ecological frames allowed Kelly to invoke a familiar rallying call for the Irish audience, that of dependency on a foreign source. This dependency would range from various supplies to nuclear expertise, while security demands would challenge the social fabric of the countryside. Kelly called for Ireland to resist the type of technocratic power which had been introduced in other EEC member states. She appealed to the Irish sense of independence to argue that the country could stand out as a type of ecological beacon for a Europe which had become engulfed in an economic and political morass. She also raised concerns about the need for democratic participation in the nuclear debate, saying the state's endorsement of Carnsore 'already demonstrates that the right to complete and objective information of every citizen is being squelched' (*ibid.*). Kelly argued that across the EEC political and scientific expedience was replacing accountability, while the true health costs of nuclear power were being withheld throughout the Community's member states. Ireland's involvement with nuclear power would also pave the way for an erosion of her traditional neutrality, with European military cooperation focusing on nuclear capabilities. Such a scenario would draw Ireland closer to membership of the North Atlantic Treaty Alliance (NATO), according to Kelly, in order to fulfil the EEC's ambitions to increase its global political power. This was being resented by anti-nuclear and pacifist groups across Europe and Kelly asked Irish citizens to join their campaign of resistance to nuclear energy. For Kelly, Ireland could still choose 'two minutes before midnight, whether or not it will accept the two headed monster – nuclear power and NATO' (*ibid.*). Kelly would subsequently go on to found the German Green party and win a seat in the European parliament.

In the aftermath of the anti-nuclear campaign calls for a public inquiry increased. The Labour Party, under pressure due to its pro-nuclear stance, called for a referendum (Baker, 1998, p. 12). Fine Gael limited itself to calling for an inquiry while adding that the concerns of the public should be addressed. While the radical left and the ITGWU opposed nuclear power, the Worker's Party continued to support the Carnsore Plant placing itself in the mainstream (*ibid.*). Fianna Fáil conceded on the public inquiry, hoping to reduce the public pressure which was building on the issue. Not for the first or last time would Fianna Fáil be caught between an economic nationalist infrastructural project and growing populist opposition. In February, Minister O'Malley announced that a public inquiry would take place. However, this did not have the desired effect, as opposition to the state's nuclear policy increased after the announcement (*ibid.*). An Interdepartmental Committee was established but again the government provided further political opportunities for the anti-nuclear movement by referring to the Committee's Report. In addition, the planned public inquiry never took place. The public felt misled on the issue, and the anti-nuclear campaigners appeared to be justified in their stance.

The summer of 1979 gave rise to plans to hold a second festival at Carnsore. This rally was more politically focused but lacked the national impact or serious media coverage of the first event (Dalby, 1998, p. 14). The second Carnsore festival called 'Return to the Point' also provided a forum for radical European groups, and some of the increased political debates led to splits and disagreements on tactics (Baker, 1990, p. 56). Three more festivals were held at Carnsore and the Irish anti-nuclear movement began to network and interact with the international movement particularly the French movement (*ibid.*).

CONCLUSION

As the state attempted to shift its energy policy in the aftermath of the oil crisis in the mid-1970s, the less than comprehensive knowledge about the links between nuclear energy and nuclear arms created a political opportunity for Irish activists to exploit. This opening in the political opportunity structure of the state allowed anti-nuclear activists to frame the issue as a moral one, thereby extending the grievance frame surrounding the issue in a way which would add pacifists, radical leftists and even the largest trades union to their list of allies. This facilitated the mobilisation process allowing a local protest in County Wexford to grow into a national movement. Due to the nature of the populist Irish political system politicians are vulnerable to the demands of the public, if these demands are mobilised in a significant and politically coherent manner, as the state attempts to accommodate vested interests (Scruggs, 1999, p. 9). Therefore, the nature of the Irish political system could be said to have facilitated the wider mobilisation of the anti-nuclear movement. As the Fianna Fáil government of 1977 had been elected on the back of a populist surge in their vote, they were vulnerable to a potential electoral backlash from the public, a concern which outweighed their desire to introduce nuclear power in Ireland.

The government eventually abandoned its plans for nuclear power, due to a series of factors including 'the Three Mile Island accident and the Kinsale gas find, combined with Des O'Malley's expulsion from the party' (Walsh, 2006). However, the Carnsore anti-nuclear protests were also a factor in the reversal of the government's nuclear energy policy, a significant victory for any social movement. The ITGWU would ultimately go into neo-corporatist 'social partnership' in the 1990s with Fianna Fail. But many groups such as Friends of the Earth continued to be active, particularly on University campuses.

By the 1980s the global Campaigns for Nuclear Disarmament (CND) would become a major political voice against nuclear arms proliferation. Despite the Chernobyl disaster in 1986 and the end of the Cold War, nuclear power has again come to the fore, ironically, as an environmentally friendly alternative to fossil fuels in the post-Gulf War era. A Forfas Report in April 2006 also indicated that the nuclear option may have to be considered by future governments as Ireland's dependency on external, fossil-based fuels will become unsustainable, while Dr. Edward Walsh of the University of Limerick has argued that Ireland might need 'a cluster of nuclear plants' to deal with any impending fuel crisis resulting from the decline of fossil fuels (Walsh, 2006). The advocacy campaign of Adi Roche and Ali Hewson, who ran the Chernobyl Children's Fund and bring children affected by the Chernobyl disaster for recuperation with Irish families serves as a reminder of the perils of nuclear power. It may be some time before people are willing to consider the nuclear option as a future energy policy for Ireland, despite the UK government's plans to redevelop

Sellafield as a potential site for the next phase of their nuclear energy production.

The campaign against the nuclear option continues in Ireland. The Irish branch of Friends of the Earth (FOE) was linked to a wider campaign to mobilise 'One Million Europeans against Nuclear Power'. They claim that Europe's governments are wasting taxpayers' money to protect a dangerous and expensive technology.

Twenty years after the Chernobyl disaster, nuclear power remains the most dangerous mechanism for electricity generation. Nuclear energy is also no solution to climate change. And, globalised terrorism makes nuclear power stations and the uncontrolled proliferation of nuclear material a serious security hazard (www.foe.ie).

Irish FOE also put forward the following arguments against nuclear power, claiming that nuclear power:

- Emits as much as much CO_2 over the whole life-cycle from fuel mining to waste management and decommissioning as a modern gas-fired power plant.
- Is insanely expensive and wouldn't survive without taxpayers' subsidies.
- Risks serious accidents with radioactive release. There have been at least 22 since the Chernobyl disaster in 1986.
- Still creates dangerous waste for many generations to come.
- Relies for fuel on uranium, the known reserves of which will run out in 50 years if nuclear energy production is maintained at current level.
- Risks nuclear proliferation, as we can't present nuclear energy as the solution to energy demand and climate change and then seek to prevent Asian, African and Latin America countries developing it (*ibid.*).

The issue remains a controversial one in Ireland, as peak oil creates further debate about sustainable futures. However, it would seem that the protests at Carnsore Point, for some the birthplace of the Irish environmental movement, remains a definitive moment for many in Irish energy policy and for its society.

REFERENCES

Baker, S. (1990). Irish environment. In W. Rudig *Green politics one*. Southern Illinios Press.

Baker, S. (1998). The nuclear issue in Ireland: The role of the Irish nuclear Movement. *Irish Political Studies*, *3*, 3–17.

Beck, U. (1996). *Risk society: Towards a new modernity*. London: Sage.

Bookchin, M. (1980). *Towards an ecological society*. Montreal: Black Rose.

Bookchin, M. (1995). *Renchanting humanity*. London: Cassele.

Carroll, J., & Kelly, P. (1980). *A nuclear Ireland?* Dublin: Transport and General Workers Union.

Dalby, S. (1998). The nuclear syndrome victory for the Irish anti-nuclear power movement. *Dublin Dawn Train No. 3*, Winter.

Dryzek, J. (1997). *The politics of the earth: Environmental discourses*. Oxford: Oxford University Press.

Green Party of Ireland. (2007). *Previous generation: Ten reasons why nuclear power makes no sense for Ireland Dublin*. Green Party of Ireland 2007 Election Manifesto.

Kriesi, H., Koopmans, R., Duyvendak, J. W., & Giugni, M. (1995). *New social movements in Western Europe. A comparative analysis*. Minneapolis, MN: University of Minnesota Press.

Leonard, L. (2008). *The environmental movement in Ireland*. Dordrecht: Springer. doi:10.1007/978-1-4020-6812-6

O'Riordan, T. (1981). *Environmentalism*. London: Pion Zedn.

Pepper, D. (1993). *Modern environmentalism: An introduction*. London: Routledge.

Scruggs, L. (1999). Institutions and environmental performance in 17 Western democracies. *British Journal of Political Studies*. Cambridge: Cambridge University Press.

Szasz, A. (2007). *Shopping our way to safety: How we changed from protecting our environment to protecting ourselves*. London: Minnesota Press.

Walsh, E. (2006). Nuclear energy: The safest of all. *Irish Times*, April 29.

Weale, A. (1992). *The new politics of pollution*. Manchester: Manchester University Press.

CHAPTER 7

CRIME☆

ABSTRACT

A number of incidents and community movements in the post-economic growth era have come to shape understandings of the Republic of Ireland's marginalized groupings. These groups exist in both urban streetscapes and rural communities; all have come to represent a new culture of transgressive resistance in a state that has never completely dealt with issues of political legitimacy or extensive poverty, creating a deviant form of 'liquid modernity' which provides the space for such groupings to exist. This chapter demonstrates that the prevailing ideology in contemporary, post-downturn Ireland have created the conditions for incidents of 'cultural criminology' that at times erupt into episodes of counter-hegemonic street level governmentality.

The chapter further argues that these groups which have emerged may represent the type of transgressive Foucaultian governmentality envisaged by Kevin Stenson, while they are indicative of subcultures of discontent and nascent racism, which belie the contented findings of various affluence and contentment surveys conducted during the years of rapid growth. The chapter develops this theme of counter-hegemonic 'governmentality', or the regional attempts to challenge authorities by local groups of transgressors. The chapter finally argues that, in many ways, the emergence of a culture of criminality in the Irish case, and media depictions of the same can be said to stem from the corruption of that country's elites as much as from any agenda for resistance from its beleaguered subcultures.

Keywords: Cultural criminology; counter-hegemonic governmentality; economic growth and downturn; marginality; Irish state

INTRODUCTION

This chapter will outline an understanding of cultures of crime as they exist in the contemporary Irish case. This understanding will incorporate existing

☆Parts of this chapter were published in Leonard (2014).

understandings of crime culture as detailed by key theorists such as Ferrell, Hayward and Young, and applied to the cultural shifts that have occurred in Ireland over a period of rapid economic and social change. This form of accelerated change has occurred within the context of the wider fluctuations of a globalized world. This form of cyclical economic growth has impacted on social change and ultimately criminality in a changing Ireland. In many ways, it has been the erudite criminologist Jock Young who has best captured a coherent understanding of these developments from a sociological perspective. In his book *The Vertigo of Late Modernity* (2007), Young details the manner in which everyday life has come to be 'disembedded' blurring the boundaries of transgression of norms and the generation of wealth or even forms of 'society'. Young locates this disconnect within a 'social exclusion thesis' (2007, p. 18); his arguments are most relevant when considering the Irish case. If we examine the changes in Irish society from Young's perspective, we can use his exclusion thesis to build verifiable findings on the cultures of criminality examined in this chapter.

Each aspect of the 'social exclusion thesis' can be applied to the Irish case with findings included:

i. *The binary*[1]: The division between a 'satisfied majority' and 'excluded and despondent minority' or minorities is evident in contemporary Irish society.
ii. *Moral exclusion*: The decline of the Catholic Church as a moral institution in the wake of abuse scandals and cover-ups by church authorities has led to a crisis in the area of moral leadership in an Ireland already shaken by a decade of political corruption. Attendant social breakdown and family dysfunction from below underpins the corruption of these institutions.
iii. *Spatial exclusion*: Urban areas in cities such as Dublin and Limerick are displaying evidence of endemic ghettoized criminality and gang culture.
iv. *Dysfunctional underclass*: The dependency of large sections of the population on the welfare state has been exasperated by a collapsed economy, and a bourgeoning crime culture.
v. *Work and redemption*: The collapse of social and economic institutions has left the Irish underclass alienated, while those in work have seen conditions deteriorate to such extent that an anomic workforce that once built the 'Celtic Tiger' economy is now experiencing a large decline in productivity. The rewards of work, such as pay or home ownership, have been reduced to such an extent by deflationary measures that 'work' has come to be a problematic concept. Ultimately, such social and economic changes have opened the door for an increased criminality in Irish society. As the borders of inclusion and exclusion are increasingly blurred, the future of Irish society remains unclear, while the cultural criminology surrounding such changes becomes all the more discernible. These issues remain as key challenges for policy makers in Ireland for the foreseeable future (Leonard, 2014).

CULTURES OF GOVERNMENTAL CRIMINALITY

The concept of 'Cultural Criminology' outlines the understanding 'that cultural dynamics carry within them the meaning of crime'. In many ways, the perspective provided by the *Cultural Criminology* of Ferrell, Hayward and Young (2008) can be said to be indicative of the underlying mentalities of late modernity's drive towards the precipice of societal organization. Essentially, the neo-apocalyptic, post-globalized streetscapes which reflect the interface between high-tech consumerism and urban gang warfare have become the site of society's anarchic lust for kicks and power in the face of an increase in a male-dominated crime culture which has spawned a territorial play for power by the disaffected and disenfranchised. Furthermore, the ebbing of the tide of consumerism in the recessionary era has been highlighted by the plight of survivors of the flooded wastelands of Bauman's (2000) 'liquid modernity', where many struggle to find a tangible life-course or to have basic rights recognized in the midst of the decline of contemporary institutions and hierarchies:

> The new rendition of the human-rights idea disassembles hierarchies and tears apart the imagery of upward ('progressive') 'cultural evolution'. Forms of life float, meet, clash, crash ... and hive off with ... equal specific gravity. Steady and stolid hierarchies and evolutionary lines are replaced with interminable and endemically inconclusive battles of recognition; at the utmost, with eminently re-negotiable pecking orders. (Bauman, 2009)

This depiction of modernity as set out by Bauman presents a chaotic and somewhat nihilistic view of society. Essentially, he argues that the cultural criminology underpinning 'liquid modernity' can lead to episodes of local 'counter-governmentality', and that this process affects all aspects of modernity, across urban, suburban and rural settings. We can apply these to recent events in the Republic of Ireland through the lens of 'cultural criminology' as defined by Ferrell, Hayward, and Young (2008); in so doing it posits an understanding of cultural criminology from the Irish perspective. This can be further understood by developing Stenson's (2008, 2009) development of Foucault's concept into what he terms 'local governmentality' or the responses of regional groups of disaffected actors who lead transgressive or deviant groups in activities of criminality and contention.

These governmental responses are discussed in relation to the transgressive responses of those in the poorest and most alienated communities in the Irish case. This concept is further developed into an account of what the authors describe as anti-hegemonic governmentality or the transgressive impulse to resist authority by deviant or contentious groups or movements. In the post-economic boom era, this view provides a filter for understanding the prevailing events which are simmering beneath the surface of an Ireland that has never come to terms with concepts such as marginality, poverty or even an acceptance of the cultural differences underpinning poverty for its urban or rural poor.

'Governmentality' is a concept introduced by Foucault (1991) and further developed by Dean (1999) which can be applied to the various levels of governance that emanate from forms of knowledge. Stenson (2008, 2009)[2] has further developed governmentality to include an understanding of 'local governmentality' which is the governmentality derived from local knowledge, wisdom or traditions. In some circumstances, 'local' forms of governmentality can include a type of cultural control from which shape the bounds of community behaviour. Stenson has shaped understandings of governmentality theory in criminology. He has achieved this by moving beyond discourse analysis, and by emphasizing the significance of the interactions between governing from 'above' (the administrative level) and 'below' (the street), while 'highlighting the centrality of struggles for territorial dominance and sovereignty at every spatial level from the local to the global' (*ibid.*). However, we have further developed this concept here to incorporate forms of counter-hegemonic governmentality or the formation of local contentious or deviant groups who challenge perceived transgressions of local rules by the authorities in the Irish case (Leonard, 2014).

'Cultural criminology' and counter-hegemonic 'governmentality' as concepts can be combined and applied to situations where alienated groups respond to harsh social conditions and subsequent attempts at social control by the state. These responses can be seen as fragmented types of social movements, be they social, cultural or political. Ireland has witnessed the emergence of sub-criminal gangs with links to dissident paramilitaries.[3] Brotherton (2004) has studied the responses of criminal gangs to attempts at social control in the United States. This fractious lifeworld of criminality is demonstrated to reflect 'larger ideological impulses' as their activities are 'framed by society's most powerful interests' creating moral panics from 'domestic demons' (*ibid.*, p. 263). Brotherton's study also outlines the linkages made about criminal gangs which locate their activities as an emerging form of domestic terrorism. He makes the point that responses to organized crime require more than a Durkheimian intervention into the *anomie* of youth. As traditional ideologies associated with opposing concepts of neo-liberalism and the welfare state collapse in the wake of new socio-economic realities, Brotherton's study reminds us that a re-evaluation of existing socio-criminological understandings of criminality is also required.

CULTURAL CRIMINOLOGY: THE LAW OF THE STREETS

> Cities ... are the dustbins into which problems produced by globalization are dumped. They are also laboratories in which the art of living with those problems (though not of resolving them) is experimented with, put to the test, and (hopefully, hopefully ....) developed. (Bauman, 2009)[4]

Bauman's understanding of liquid modernity includes a distinction between creative and destructively routine forms of cultural expression. While the former is positive in its innovative expressiveness, the latter is seen to engender a desire for an irregular transgression of established norms in the search for freedom from the restrictiveness of hegemonic acquiescence. Cultural criminology can be seen as a pathway towards the dissolving of the 'conventional understandings and accepted boundaries' surrounding criminological depictions of societal strain. This path runs through a series of disciplines which incorporate 'urban studies, media studies ... cultural and human geography, critical theory, anthropology and social movement theory' (Ferrell et al., 2008) in a new form of reinvigorated socio-criminological criticism which sets its focus on the fallout surrounding late modernity's 'world in flux'.

Brotherton's understanding of an ideological malevolent form of embedded cultural criminology can be proportionally applied to Bauman's account of the globalized, modern city, which in the Irish case is its capital, Dublin. In June 2009 a lone female member of the Irish police force *An Garda Siochána* was assaulted by a gang of youths when she intervened in their public drinking session on a busy Dublin city centre street. The Garda was beaten, knocked to the ground and bitten on the face while a crowd gathered around the incident. None of the members of the public intervened to assist the policewoman, and one member of the gang was heard to shout 'she deserved it, she's a pig'. Some of the youths and members of the public were filming the incident on their mobile phones (*Evening Herald*, 2009). The incident was one of many which have occurred in the Republic's capital in the years following the decline of the once buoyant 'Celtic Tiger' economy (Leonard, 2014).

In truth, the poverty of inner city Dublin (once described as having slums 'worse than Calcutta's in the early 1900s) had not been caused by the international monetary deals occurring in the nearby International Financial Services Centre (IFSC), whose gleaming edifices stand literally right across the busy thoroughfare where the assault on the female Garda occurred. Rather, the cause of this endemic poverty has been the neglectful policies of successive governments, which have starved the city's neighbourhoods of investment for decades. Dublin's inner city has a third or even fourth generation heroin problem, while the majority of prisoners in the notoriously decrepit Mountjoy Prison (located a few blocks away from the IFSC) also came from these mean streets, according to Irish criminologist Paul O'Mahony's study during the socio-economic transformations of the 1990s.[5] While O'Mahony contends that the majority of those incarcerated during the 1990s were from the inner city, the demographics of these neighbourhoods have altered in the intervening decade. The majority of inhabitants of inner Dublin in 2009 were born outside of Ireland, reflecting a decade where globalization brought tens of thousands of immigrants into Ireland, a pattern which is now reversing with the economic downturn. Nonetheless, these statistics reflect a failure to integrate these new arrivals into Irish society.

The discourse of immigration has been a problematic one in Ireland. The state has led the line in the creation of an image of migrants as 'Other',[6] in Said's original understanding of the term. State officials and media reports have described migrants in populist terms, with one serving state minister causing a scandal when he dismissed those concerned with underpaid Turkish construction workers as 'kebabs' in a debate about their plight. The same minister survived to implement the harshest cuts in social welfare in the state's history. The education minister was criticized for attempting to create a school exclusively for the children of African migrants; the same minister's father was the spokesperson for the virulent pro-life lobby which has campaign for decades to deny fundamental rights to Irish women. One report was critical of a senior Irish judge, who said Roma migrants from Romania raised their children to steal and were responsible for our 'shops being robbed blind' (*Irish Times*, 2010). This populist atmosphere from elements in the state has trickled also down into the street, where migrants face racist attacks and hostility.

The 2006 Central Statistics Office (CSO) report on immigration demonstrates that in three local election wards around Dublin's main thoroughfare O'Connell Street, most of the population were born outside of Ireland. The CSO figures show that the population of the North City Ward in Dublin is now 55% foreign national and nearly one-third of these people had originally come from outside the European Union (EU). Foreign nationals had accounted for 10% of the total Irish population in 2007, with over 200,000 coming from one source, Poland. By 2008, this figure came to be reduced considerably as non-attached migrants departed. Less than half of foreign nationals assigned with Social Security Numbers (PPSNs) in 2004 had been recorded as actively working in Ireland by 2008 (CSO, 1998). There have also been accusations of discrimination against the indigenous ethnic Traveller group made against the state. The United Nation's Committee on the Elimination of Racial Discrimination 2006 report supported claims by various Traveller groups that as an ethnically separate group it suffered from discrimination (Irish *Independent*, 2010).

A report to the *Oireachtas (Parliamentary) European Affairs Committee* on immigration in Ireland needs to review its anti-discrimination laws to better protect the migrant Roma community, which faces high levels of racism and discrimination in Ireland and across Europe. According to the report, the state needed to train all public officials, civil servants and police to prevent further discrimination against this migrant group (*Irish Times*, 2010). The report estimates that up to 2500 to 3000 Roma are now living in Ireland, and goes on to indicate that this group are faced with widespread discrimination:

> The results of an EU-wide survey have shown that only 24 per cent of Irish people would be comfortable having a Roma person as their next-door neighbour and that only 6 per cent had Roma friends or acquaintances. (*ibid.*)

One area of cultural criminology with disturbingly fascistic undertones is the emergence of right wing skinhead websites with links to Ireland's semi-professional soccer clubs. These 'ultras' mimic the behaviour of British and European skinhead hooligan groups, although on a smaller scale. The groups have established a number of websites, and these were utilized to arrange clashes with rival groups, and links with external factions. Even the cultural clashes associated with Northern Ireland's sectarian troubles have spilled onto the streets of the Republic. In the spring of 2006, riots surrounding the northern loyalist 'Love Ulster' march through the streets of Dublin. While the 'Peace Process' had brought the opposing nationalists and unionists together in the Belfast Assembly, the Orange Order's tradition of marching into areas where it was not welcome had become a part of the political culture of Loyalist politics.

It was this impulse towards provocative governmentality which lay behind the controversial 'Love Ulster' march into Dublin. What transpired was an anarchistic incident of attempt at countergovernmentality; local dissident republicans, Dublin's football hooligans and some non-nationals more intent on looting than rioting attacked the parade.[7] The march was stopped and the streets of Dublin, which were full of Saturday afternoon shoppers, were briefly transformed into a scene more reminiscent of Belfast at the height of 'the Troubles'. These scenes were the worst examples of public disorder in Dublin since the 2002.

'May Day' riots, where police removed their numbers and attacked anti-globalization protestors. A number of police were subsequently brought to trial in the aftermath of clashes with protestors.

Writing in 2001, Jeff Ferrell outlines the world of the 'mean streets' of post-affluence society in urban Denver in the mid-western United States with these opening lines:

> Something's gone wrong. Something has shifted away, away, away from what it means to live our lives together in public, away from a sense of the city as an open, inclusive society. (Ferrell, 2001, p. 1)

It is interesting to note that both Ferrell's vivid account of Denver and the above-mentioned story of Dublin's crimescape come after years of rapid growth followed by the subsequent global economic crash which has come to dominate contemporary culture. These urban wastelands provide the settings for the fragmented lifestyles outlined by Bauman's (2000) concept of a contemporary modernity where the marginalized attempt to renegotiate their uncertain existence from crisis to crisis. This post-modern landscape reflects a form of hyper-pluralism', as new cultural contests are borne from the dissenting voices of the identity-based culture wars which have come to supersede class struggle in the post-modern moment. The emergence of neo-conservative political policies has also been reflected in the response to new cultural patterns. In addition, the collapse of the globalized financial sector is but one more reminder of the ongoing demise of existing institutional orders which have separated a privileged elite (the 1% owning 40% of US wealth for instance) from a bourgeoning army of marginalized poor, addicted, undocumented or trafficked victims of a corrupt version of globalization.[8]

Essentially, the poorest inhabitants of cities like Dublin and Denver never benefited from the growth that is reflected in the expansive urban skylines that rise around them. For example, despite the hubris surrounding the much vaunted neo-liberal successes which characterized the 'Celtic Tiger' boom years in Ireland, poverty levels remained endemic. In addition, the lucrative subsidies to developers in Denver outlined by Ferrell (2001, pp. 38–39) were mirrored in Dublin and across Ireland. However, rates of homelessness and subsequent lawlessness increased in both jurisdictions at this time. In America, tent cities are emerging for the contemporary victims of foreclosures, echoing the 'Hoovervilles' of the 1930s. In Ireland, where up to 22% of 18–25 year old are unemployed, the traditional social safety valve of emigration has again become common.

Kevin Hayward further examines the 'spatial dynamics of exclusion' that exist in the city (2004, pp. 155–167). By applying Papastergiadis and Rodgers' (1996) concept of 'parafunctional' urban spaces to the dynamics underpinning episodes of contemporary criminology, Hayward set out to understand the reclamation of the wasteland or street by the disaffected and the disenfranchised. Culturally, a brave new world of 24 hour news media and pop culture has embraced the new culture of criminology for its entertainment value and its sensationalist aspect. This saturation of criminological cultural production has become a sideshow within Baudrillard's (1994) post-modern simulacra, as the contradictions of subversive resistance and the corruption of authority are merged into what the authors describe as a 'cultural motion'. These criminal-cultural patterns are captured and reproduced in hazer's mobile phones, CCTV cameras, news broadcasts and on episodes of 'crime TV'. Under this conceptualization, the public space comes to represent no more than a post-modernist venue for territorial disputes; it was one such territorial conflict that marked the site of the attack on the young Irish policewoman in Dublin. In the culture of the disaffected, hostility and apathy to violence run side by side, as the quest for local governmentality remains a continual and fluid struggle for all involved in the contest for power in the fractured public spaces.

A number of public protests have broken out sporadically in Ireland since the turn of the Millenium. The presence of the high number of police in rural areas with no known record of crime, as has happened at the 'Shell to Sea' pipeline dispute, or at anti – 'Water charges' or 'Bin charges', has given rise to accusations of 'political policing' being directed at the authorities. The Corrib gas dispute took on a new dimension, as protestors were badly man-handled by police as a form of regional counter-hegemonic governmentality was exercised by the protestors, whose own political agendas went far beyond the gas pipeline issue.

The transformation and redeployment of police in this case reflects ongoing concerns 'that state criminal justice has moved too far away from the concerns of ordinary people – it has become too distant, too out of touch, insufficiently reflective of different social groups in society' (Shapland, 2008, p. 1).[9] In the absence of community confidence due to an erosion of state legitimation, sporadic episode of 'countergovernmentality' can emerge, as witnessed in the Rossport campaign. The '*Shell to Sea*' campaign, which began as a dispute about an onshore gas pipeline, extended into counter-governmental episodes which witnessed local farmers being imprisoned for refusing to accept the pipeline on their land (Leonard, 2008).

Over the years since the economy went into decline and the campaign of 'the Rossport 5' erupted, criminal activity has come to dominate the western city of Limerick, 200 mile south of rural Mayo. Here, violent disputes between two rival gangs from the Moyross section of the city turned the city on its head, with an assortment of murders, extortion threats, kidnappings and intimidation of witnesses dominating the television and print media. Sociologist Niamh Hourigan has studied the culture of intimidation surrounding Limerick gangland violence. In her view, sending gang leaders to prison doesn't reduce the extent of their own distorted brand of counter-hegemonic governmentality:

> Imprisoning serious criminals does undoubtedly constrain gang members' capacity for action but it does not eliminate it entirely because of the continuing supply of teenage gang members on the outside willing to carry out commands. More importantly, at the base of this criminal hierarchy is a small army of juveniles who engage in continuing campaigns of intimidation aimed at local residents which effectively maintain the 'rule of the gangs' on a daily basis in pockets of Limerick and West Dublin. (Hourigan, 2010)

In the wake of the intimidation of witnesses and the murder of innocent victims of Limerick's gang wars, the state introduced non-jury trials for gang-related activities through the *Offenses against the State Act* 2008. The legislation, which had been used against paramilitaries active in the Republic during Northern Ireland's 'Troubles', has now been directed at individuals associated directly with gangland activities. Under the Act, individual officers of any rank can testify that a gang member poses a threat, and this can be used to delay the release of that individual. The Act was criticized by Human Rights groups as it suspended the common law right of trial by jury to individuals.

The rise of Ireland's criminal gangs and increased drug dealing has led to internal disputes, gang shootings and violence across Dublin city. The emergence of major drugs gangs has caused difficulties for the authorities, as many in Dublin became addicted to hard drugs such as heroin. With the death and arrest of major criminal leaders after the shooting of journalist Veronica Guerin in 1996, smaller and often more violent gangs took the place of subversives as the most sought-after by Irish authorities. Gang shootings have become a regular occurrence in Dublin as these gangs fight for ascendancy and control of the lucrative drugs market.

Policing in rural areas has been an area of concern on occasion in Ireland, leading to the establishment of the Morris Tribunal of Inquiry. Irish criminologist Vicky Conway has examined issues in rural policing and Morris in her 2010 study *The Blue Wall of Silence: The Morris Tribunal and Police Accountability in*

Ireland. The questionable activities in the Donegal region led to a landmark tribunal of inquiry:

> In October 2008, after six years, the Morris Tribunal completed its work. Its findings catalogued corruption, negligence, misconduct, and 'a blue wall of silence' in *An Garda Siochana*, on an unprecedented scale. The reports also highlight the inadequacies of existing accountability systems that were reformed substantially mid-way through the work of the Tribunal, by the Garda Siochana Act 2005. (Conway, 2010)

According to Conway, the Tribunal found that 'without substantial reform, the activities documented could reoccur elsewhere in Ireland'. While the police enjoy good levels of support amongst the Irish public, the onset of regional episodes of political policing or corrupt practices remains a concern.

THE FAILING STATE: A TAXONOMY OF NEGLECT AND ABUSE

In November 2009, the Irish state introduced what has been described by commentators as 'the most right wing in the nation's history'. The budget, which created the National Assets Management Bureau (NAMA) to refinance the banking sector and provide credit to the bankrupt property-development lobby, was further condemned as being 'anti-poor', as taxes on low earners and social welfare cuts for the poor and disabled[10] were introduced by the Fianna Fáil-Green Party coalition government to fund the bailout. From a governance perspective, the Irish state has a long-standing history of failing its poorest classes. In many ways, the state exported the problem through the siphon of emigration to the United States and United Kingdom since independence was achieved in 1922. In Ireland, the poor were to be seen and not heard, as the tradition working class protections of trade unions and left wing politics were lost amid the dominant hubris of post-colonial nationalism and clerical triumphalism.

This culture of antagonism to the poor can be traced back to the landgrabbing days of the Famine of the 1840s, when a million Irish poor died of starvation and disease while a million more left for Britain or America. And while it was the inner city poor of Dublin who marched out in support of the 1913 Worker's Lock Out and the 1916 Easter Rebellion, their lot under the Irish Free State which was set up in 1922 was not much better than conditions had been under the rule of the Crown. The harsh poverty and mass emigration of the 1930s, 1950s and 1980s is now being revisited in the late 2000s, with the addition of the complexities of a newly multicultural society adding to the array of issues which are being affected by the Irish state's inability to deal with issues of poverty in any kind of meaningful way.

One result of the painful birth pangs of the state-witnessed counter-governmental groupings persists in Ireland, creating episodes of Habermasian

'Legitimation Crisis' as neo-republican splinter groups and criminal gangs have challenged the authority of the state at various periods during its history. While the successful co-optation of the mainstream republican movement from terrorism into government has been completed in Northern Ireland, the legitimacy of the state has never been fully accepted or extended out towards many of its poorest classes.

During the 'Troubles' which afflicted the North armed robberies and kidnappings were commonplace in the Republic.

These subversive activities have given way to robberies by criminal gangs which operated in the grey areas of the underworld which were also populated by republican terrorists and those on the peripheries of the 'black economy'. The response of successive Ministers of Justice was a form of class-based political policing aimed at targeting the republicans and criminal gangs in a manner which led to a deviation from the traditional community-based policing of *An Garda Siochána* into a form of policing for the political and propertied classes. The subsequent revelations of systemic corruption between Ireland's largest political party Fianna Fáil and various property developers has added to the malaise surrounding politics in the Republic, following the economic collapse and International Monetary Fund (IMF) bailout since 2008 (Leonard & Kenny, 2011).

A CULTURE OF INSTITUTIONAL ABUSE

May (2009) saw the publication of the *Ryan Report* into the physical and sexual abuse of children who had been in the care of various Catholic Orders in a number of institutions around the country from the 1930s through to the 1990s. The fact that many of the children taken into care were basically abducted from their working class parents by a church that was given impunity by the state is shocking enough. However, the Roman Catholic Church still retains control over more than 90% of the primary schools in the Irish state is indicative of the extent of control that institution continues to wield in the Irish state. While these reports were met with revulsion in Irish society, public responses to the findings were somewhat muted. However, the *One in Four* campaign organized by survivors of child-sexual abuse was prominent in mobilizing public support for these investigations, demonstrating the significance of rights-watch groups in exposing corruption.

The fact that the Religious Orders involved resisted attempts to pay adequate amounts of compensation to the victims belies the culture of hostility exercised by the elite classes in the Republic over its poor since its inception. Subsequent reports have included allegations of collusion between senior clerics and the police, including the non-prosecution and protection of abusive priests. In December 2009, some senior figures from the Catholic Church were forced to resign after allegations of cover-ups in cases involving clerical child abuse after allegations of cover-ups emerged in the *Murphy Commission Report*. The denial of human rights to Ireland's poor is reflective of Bauman's understanding of modernity in crisis.

Corruption in Irish politics and society is endemic and all-persuasive. From Prime Ministers to priests, and from bankers and property developers to the spineless 'managers' of the state's bureaucracy, all concerns for values, rights or truths have been corrupted through a maelstrom of spin, conjecture and lies which are offered up to excuse all manner of personal or cultural aggrandizement by the state's ruling 'elite'. On the city streets corroded by neglect or in the rural communities threatened by inappropriate or aggressive development, local populations are depicted as transgressors when their attempts to negotiate or resist the projects and agendas of these corrupt elites become a threat to 'progress'.

In her study *Political Corruption in Ireland 1922–2010: A Crooked Harp?*, Elaine Byrne (2012) outlines the erosion of political ethics and behaviour since the foundation of the Irish state in 1922, right through to the emergence of the International Monetary Fund (IMF) in Irish internal affairs. This intervention followed the loss of Irish economic sovereignty in 2010. Byrne argues that, in the Irish case, understandings of corruption evolve, and this evolution mirrors the changing contours of state behaviour. Most of the major institutions in Irish society such as the political sector, the banks, the religious sector, higher education and large sections of industry are inherently corrupt, racked with an insidious form of conservatism and cronyism that is as incestuous as it is hostile to external examination.

In contemporary Ireland, the creation of a transgressive social 'other' has targeted those excluded from the centralized core of power; community activists, environmental campaigners, anti-globalization protestors have been targeted, arrested and imprisoned during an era when all of the main social institutions including senior members of the majority Fianna Fáil party, a range of clerics from all sectors of the Catholic Church, senior bank officials and figures from indigenous businesses have all been implicated in major cases of corruption and abuse of power. Nonetheless, the criminal justice resources of the state still target those afflicted by addiction and poverty or those who resist political hegemony in defence of communities, rather than investigating the endemic corruption which blights contemporary Irish society at every level.

CONCLUSION

With the decline of institutions which had shaped Irish society for so long, post-modern Ireland is at the crossroads. Politically, most movements have been co-opted into existing structures of power. The Greens became the minority partner in a centre-right coalition; the trade unions have been enfeebled by their participation in the state's corporatist 'social partnership' model while even the traditionally subversive *Sinn Fein* party, once the political wing of the Irish Republican Army (IRA), sat in coalition with the religious fundamentalist and social conservative Democratic Unionist Party in Northern Ireland's ruling Assembly. In summer 2017, the DUP and Teresa May's Conservative part have formed a controversial coalition in Westminster, in breach of the tenets of the Good Friday Agreement. In the wake of such endemic political co-optation, opportunities for a coherent political alternative have become restricted, limiting moves to create formal political opposition to the mainstream, with the void filled by counter-hegemonic 'governmental' activity which is underpinned with varying degrees of criminality. Moreover, Ireland's population have become socially sated by years of rampant consumerism fuelled by the affluence of the 'Celtic Tiger' decade economic growth. The economic downturn, coming in the wake of persistent political and social scandals, has left the Irish public angry and shell-shocked, with emigration, forgotten for a generation, now once again rising.

Youth culture in Ireland is in many ways reflective of the detached, consumerism of mainstream society. Drug use, binge-drinking and the culture of joyriding 'boy-racers' dominate the scene both in urban and rural settings. This activity is underpinned by a rise in suicides by young people, mostly amongst males (Maclachlan & Smyth, 2005). Irish post-modernist popular culture is discussed by Balzano, Mulhall, and Moynagh (2007), with issues of post-colonialism, sexuality and community psychology being applied to existing and emerging forms of Irish identity in the era of globalization. And it is from the chaos of this fluctuating, liquid society that some positive cultural initiatives are manifesting themselves among the post-affluent social fragments, as mutually supporting support groups for youth suicide, teen pregnancies, drug and alcohol addiction and alternative sexualities emerge to fill the void left by the collapse of mainstream society.

However, the depictions of young people in the Irish media are often sensationalistic and prurient. The media in Ireland rarely investigate underlying issues which are contributory factors to levels of endemic poverty amongst Ireland's most marginal sectors. However, sensationalist headlines about welfare fraud by unmarried mothers or asylum seekers have featured heavily in media reportage. This 'moral panic' approach to reporting crime has in itself influenced responses to crime. In addition, sensationalist reporting of crime has fed into the politicalization of policing, as successive justice ministers have used populist 'law and order' approaches to tackling crime in order to bolster their political standing. This correlation between politics, media and crime is a distorted form of hegemony, as Irish media comes to be influenced by US and UK media coverage of crime, Irish political responses to crime have been shaped by a populist right-wing ideology that places no emphasis on restoration or rehabilitation. We have seen how this correlates with Young's 'Moral

Exclusion Thesis', as various institutions corrode and become closed in the aftermath of decades of corruption and cronyism. This distortion of institutions has subsequently led to an ideological morass that frames contemporary debates about crime and society in post-bailout Ireland.

NOTES

1. Adapted from Young (2007, p. 18).

2. The development of the concept of anti-hegemonic 'governmentality' put forward in this chapter has its origins in Stenson's own interpretation of the notion of 'governmentality', and must be acknowledged. Dean's work has also shaped my thinking on the parameters of this Foucaultian idea, which the authors have combined with their own perceptions of social movement contention and Irish sociology, politics and history.

3. Criminal gangs have linked with dissident paramilitaries to secure weapons, and activities have overlapped in some cases.

4. While Bauman is writing about London, his illustration of globalized urban breakdown is applicable in the case of Ireland's cities, and to Dublin, with its problems of poverty and drugs crime, in particular.

5. We can further understand responses to the crimescapes of urban modernity by examining justice-related social movements in a manner put forward by writers such as Braithwaite (1998), Young (2007) and Hoyle, Young, and Hill (2002).

6. Said (1979).

7. *Irish Times*, February 27, 2006.

8. Leonard and Kenny (2010).

9. Attempts by the Centre for Public Inquiry (CPI), a rights-watch group, to investigate the *Shell to Sea* case and other episodes of corruption in Ireland led to the CPI being closed down after interventions by the state.

10. The Fianna Fáil/Green Party coalition cut funding to the blind, to Crumlin Children's Hospital and reduced teaching assistants for disabled and disadvantaged children to fund its bailout of the banking and property-development sectors.

REFERENCES

Balzano, W., Mulhall, A., & Moynagh, S. (Eds.). (2007). *Irish postmodernisms and popular culture*. London: Palgrave Macmillan.

Baudrillard, J. (1994). *SIMULACRA and simulation*. Ann Arbor, MI: The University of Michigan Press.

Bauman, Z. (2000). *Liquid modernity*. London: Polity.

Bauman, Z. (2009). Culture in a globalised city. *Occupied London, 3*. Retrieved from http://www.occupiedlondon.org/bauman

Braithwaite, J. (1998). Restorative justice. In M. Tonry (Ed.). *The handbook of crime and punishment* (pp. 323–344). New York, NY: Oxford University Press.

Brotherton, D. (2004). *What happened to the pathological gang? Notes from a case study on the Latin Kings and Queens in New York*. In Ferrell.

Byrne, E. (2012). *Political corruption in Ireland 1922–2010: A crooked harp?* Manchester: Manchester University Press.

Central Statistics Office. (1998). *Quarterly national household survey crime and victims* (September–November). Dublin: C.S.O.

Conway, V. (2010). *The blue wall of silence: The Morris Tribunal and police accountability in Ireland*. Dublin: Irish Academic Press.

Dean, M. (1999). *Governmentality: Power and rule in modern society*. London: Sage.

Evening Herald. (2009). Savage attack on woman Garda. *Dublin: Evening Herald/Independent Newspapers*, June 20, 2009.

Ferrell, J. (2001). *Tearing down the streets: Adventures in urban anarchy*. London: Palgrave.

Ferrell, J., Hayward, K., & Young, J. (2008). *Cultural criminology: An invitation*. London: Sage.

Foucault, M. (1991). Governmentality. In G. Burchell, C. Gordon, & P. Miller (Eds). *The Foucault effect: Studies in governmentality* (pp. 87–104). Chicago, IL: University of Chicago Press.

Hourigan, N. (2010). *Understanding limerick: Social exclusion and change*. Cork: Cork University Press. (in print).

Hoyle, C., Young, R., & Hill, R. (2002). *Proceed with caution: An evaluation of the Thames Valley police initiative in restorative cautioning*. York: Joseph Rowntree Foundation.

Irish Independent. (2010). State paid out €130m in funding to Travellers UN asks Ireland to prove it is not a racially discriminating country. *Dublin: Independent Newspapers*, January 3, 2010.

Irish Times. (2006). Dublin's descent into violent chaos. *Dublin: Irish Times Ltd.*, February 27, 2006.

Irish Times. (2010). Anti-Roma racism focused on by report. *Dublin: Irish Times Ltd.*, January 2, 2010.

Leonard, L. (2008). *The environmental movement in Ireland*. Dordrecht: Springer.

Leonard, L. (2014). Cultural criminology, governmentality and the liquidity of the failing state: The view from Ireland. *Critical Criminology*, *22*(2), 293–306, doi:10.1007/s10612-013-9217-0

Leonard, L., & Kenny, P. (2010). Review of cultural criminology: An invitation by Ferrell, Hayward and Young. *Theoretical Criminology*, *14*(1).

Leonard, L., & Kenny, P. (2011). Power, corruption and lies: Irish political, economic and social policy': 1900–2011. In L. Leonard & I. Botetzagias (Eds.), *Sustainable politics and the crisis of the peripheries: Ireland and Greece* (Vol. 8, pp. 25–44). Advances in Ecopolitics. Bingley: Emerald Group Publishing Limited.

Maclachlan, M., & Smyth, C. (Eds.). (2005). *Binge drinking & youth culture: Alternative perspectives*. Dublin: Liffey Press.

Papastergiadis, N., & Rodgers, H. (1996). Parafunctional spaces. In J. Stathatos (Ed.), *Art and the city*. London: Academy Group.

Ryan, S. (2009). *The commission to inquire into child abuse*. Dublin: Government Publications.

Said, E. (1979). *Orientalism*. New York, NY: Vintage Books.

Shapland, J. (Ed). (2008). *Justice, community and civil society*. London: Willan.

Stenson, K. (2008). Surveillance and sovereignty. In M. Deflem (Ed.), *Surveillance and governance, sociology of crime, law and deviance* (Vol. 10, pp. 281–303). Bingley: Emerald Group Publishing Limited.

Stenson, K. (2009). Crime, conflict, sovereignty and the struggle for governance from below. Paper to the 5th all-Ireland criminology conference, University College Dublin, Dublin.

Young, J. (2007). *The vertigo of late modernity*. London: Sage.

CHAPTER 8

MULTICULTURALISM

ABSTRACT

The emergence of a multicultural and diverse society in the Republic of Ireland should be reflected in the nation's justice system. This chapter examines how community policing and restorative justice policy and practice can be developed to reflect these new cultural realities. It focuses on the challenges faced by those training to participate in frontline services in the justice system with an increasingly diverse population. These issues are examined in the context of the trend towards restorative justice initiatives, with a focus on the challenges facing those in the justice system and civil society who must provide a form of training which is cognisant of increased diversity and multiculturalism.

Keywords: Multiculturalism; diversity; restorative justice; community policing; training; conference

INTRODUCTION

The legal system of any state provides the framework for the legislation for equality and diversity.[1] Moreover, and perhaps just as importantly, the legislative framework of the state provides a wider sense of the state's approach towards multiculturalism and the promotion of equality and perspectives on diversity. In the Republic of Ireland, the legal system remains independent of direct political interference, within the contexts of the pluralistic guidelines set out in the Constitution. The state has published a *National Action Plan against Racism (NPAR): Planning for Diversity* (2005). This action plan set out the parameters of an intercultural society in Ireland. In addition, the rights of all citizens are also constitutionally protected. Therefore, while the authority of the state is legitimised through the legal frameworks which establish certain rights, the rights of its citizens to participate in politics and civil society and the protection and promotion of these indelible rights is also secured by these legislative structures.

In addition, Ireland's migratory data is constantly changing. While many immigrants make Ireland their home, others may leave to seek opportunities elsewhere, as the Irish have done over the centuries. These shifts can be seen in international studies. According to Titley and Maguire:

> The recent International Organization for Migration (IOM) thematic study, Migration and the Economic Crisis in the European Union, contains an overview of the situation in Ireland. The picture this report paints is of sharp decreases in immigration from new European Member States since 2008, out-migration by former immigrants, and, overall, the return of negative net migration. But, importantly, many of the migrants who came to Ireland in the previous ten to fifteen years are not leaving. (Maguire & Titley, 2010)

RACISM IN IRELAND

According to a report of the European Network Against Racism (ENAR), there was an increase in racially motivated assaults in Ireland in the final six months of 2015. These included a number of serious assaults that led to injury, according to the report. These numbers are at a record level, and are drawn from over 40 organisations across Ireland.[2] This increase in violence against immigrants occurred at a time when the Council of Europe's Committee on Human Rights criticised the Irish government for violating Irish Traveller's human rights by not providing them with adequate accommodation as they required (Holland, 2016).

In a joint court action taken by Irish Traveller and European Romany groups, the Irish government was found to have been neglecting its responsibilities in relation to Traveller housing. Funding for Travellers had been significantly reduced in recent years, according to the groups. Ireland was found to be in breach of Traveller rights by not providing families with full 'social legal and economic protection' (*ibid.*). The European Committee found that there was also insufficient standards of accommodation for Traveller groups in Ireland.

The ENAR report found that the group had received 165 reports of racist incidents for in the months July to December 2015. These included incidents such as 'racist public and sexual harassment, online abuse, discrimination in employment and service, and other attacks' (Flaherty, 2016). Ireland's criminal justice system was also struggling to deal with the increase in racism. The next section will examine conferencing as a potential solution to multicultural and intercultural disputes, an approach to social justice which can take all cultural backgrounds into consideration.

CONFERENCING

In the past, the formal criminal justice system has been overly focused on what O'Mahony (2001, p. 11) calls, 'public interest' which effectively amounted to the state overriding the interests of the other stakeholders, including ethnic groups. Conferencing on the other hand is, as Consedine advocates, a 'philosophy that embraces a wide range of human emotions including healing, mediation, compassion, forgiveness, mercy, reconciliation as well as sanction when appropriate' (Consedine, 1995, p. 183). Conferencing, in Consedine's view, offers a process whereby those affected by criminal behaviour, be they victims, offenders, the families involved or the wider community, all have a part to play. With conferencing, victims and offenders assume central roles and the state takes a back seat. The process does not focus on vengeance and punishment but seeks to heal both the community and the individuals involved. This is achieved by a process that puts the notion of reparation, not punishment, at its centre.[3] In the following section the key features of conferencing and indicate its usefulness in the context of diversity and multiculturalism are outlined.

One area where issues of justice and diversity intersect is that of minorities and drug abuse. The National Advisory Committee on Drugs (NACD) set out its strategy in its submission to the Health Service Executive's (HSE) *National Intercultural Strategy* in 2007. The NACD submission acknowledges the particularly vulnerable status of those sections of the population of diverse cultural and ethnic backgrounds. The NACD document recognises the particular risks of social exclusion faced by Travellers,[4] asylum seekers, refugees and migrant workers. Minority groups face heightened economic and social disadvantage, increasing the risks of drug abuse due to problems in nine key areas: 'education, health, crime, employment, housing, previous and current drug use, family, social networks and the environment'.[5] Highlighting these risks should not be used to label or stigmatise minority groups, but the difficulties associated with social marginalisation and exclusion resulting from underdeveloped infrastructure for multiculturalism needs to be acknowledged, and tackled.

The National Drugs Strategy, 2001–2008 represents one response to the requirement for an integrated approach to issues such as drug addiction within the context of the marginalisation of some ethnic groups. The success of any such approach will be contingent on the ability of state bodies and civil society to deal with the marginalisation of minority groups, as well as dealing with the wider issues surrounding drug abuse nationally. One method of coping with this lack of engagement would be to develop enhanced training programmes for all relevant state and civil society agencies in dealing with equality, diversity and the problems associated with social exclusion due to the lack of effective multicultural policies and practices across the services. In order for such training to be effective, a multi-agency approach would be required. Stereotyping and negative profiling of ethnic groups would have to be challenged and replaced with better understanding of the requirements of a range of ethnic groups within the Irish context.[6] For instance, racism in Ireland may take the form of 'white versus white' intolerance, in addition to the 'white versus black' model associated with the Anglo-American experience. We argue that with effective training, a form of 'cultural competence' would be established, reflecting the ability of the state and civil society to address the requirements of an increasingly ethnically diverse society. This would lead to greater cultural awareness and sensitivity within general society, leading in turn to the creation of greater confidence in minority groups in the competency of state and civil society to effectively and sensitively deal with the requirements of a diverse and multicultural society (Sangster, Shiner, Patel, & Sheikh, 2002).

Conferencing requires training which is sensitive to different cultures. The most significant aspects of any competency-based training must underpin the importance of frontline interventions in the overlapping areas of justice, vulnerability and diversity. The cultural aspects of this social and criminological milieu should be reflected in such interventions, by targeting outcomes across the range of issues, and by preparing practitioners to recognise and build on the cultural indicators that emerge during moments of social crisis. One initiative which may succeed in embracing diversity while addressing the need for redress is conferencing.

Conferencing has been established to engage the accused, the victim and the practitioner in a process of emotive exchanges, based on functional interactions which produce outcomes such as Braithwaite's seminal concept of 'reintegrative shaming'. However, we argue in this chapter that such approaches may not work in cases of the vulnerable, or certain ethnic groupings, as the emotive exchange which is produced through restorative events may prove to be counterproductive.

RESOLVING ETHNIC CONFLICTS

In general, the conferencing philosophy is based on three beliefs:

1. Crime results in harm to victims, offenders and communities.
2. Not only Government but also victims, offenders and communities should be actively involved in the criminal justice process.
3. In promoting justice, the Government should be responsible for preserving order (Van Ness & Strong, 1997).

These general beliefs lead to a number of common elements among restorative justice programmes. The key features of the concept of restorative justice can be outlined as follows:

> It is a process whereby parties with a stake in a specific offence resolve collectively how to deal with the aftermath of the offence and its implications for the future. It is a problem-solving approach to crime, which involves the parties themselves, and the community generally in an active relationship with statutory agencies. It seeks to balance the concerns of the victim and the community with the need to reintegrate the offender into society. It seeks to assist recovery of the victim and enable all parties with a stake in the justice process to participate in it. (Aertson, 2000, p. 14)

Braithwaite (1989) has been to the forefront in the study of conferencing, especially through the means of his concept of 'reintegrative shaming'. He contends that there are many reasons for the criminal justice system failing in its efforts to control levels of crime such as the stigmatisation of criminals. Braithwaite's theory of 'reintegrative shaming' holds that it is the societies with the lowest crime rates that have the ability to shame criminal conduct most effectively (Braithwaite in Johnstone et al., 2003), as there is an important difference between shaming a person and stigmatising them.[7] Training practitioners to deal with 'reintegrative shaming' includes preparing councillors to understand that disapproving of the wrong of the act while treating the person as essentially good is a significant aspect of restorative practice. Reintegrative shaming in summary relates to a strong disapproval of the act but conveying and articulating a response that is seen to respect the offender Braithwaite (1989).

Practitioners must also be prepared to deal with victims of different ethnic backgrounds and cultures, and restorative justice aims to restore social support through institutionalising the gathering around familiar cultural mores during a time of crisis Braithwaite (1989). This can reduce racial tensions by removing the sense of insecurity and disempowerment of both victims and offenders through a process of deliberative societal democracy. Proper training for racial integration through restorative justice can design institutions so that concerns about issues like unemployment have a channel through which they can flow from discussions about local injustices up to national economic policy making debates (Braithwaite citied in Johnstone et al., 2003). Braithwaite (2003) doesn't advocate that society abolishes the concept of crime or the key elements of state criminal justice systems which have been globalised, rather he believes in shifting power from them to civil society, retaining key elements but shifting power away from central institutions and checking power that remains by deliberative democracy from below, for example self-regulatory practice which restorative justice enables (Braithwaite cited in Tonry, 1998).

Daly (2003) in her article on 'Restorative Justice: the real story' addresses the problem of defining restorative justice-based conferencing. She states that this is not easily done as it encompasses a variety of practices at different stages of the criminal justice process. She also points out that, in virtually all legal contexts involving individual criminal matters, restorative justice practices have only been applied to those offenders who have admitted to an offence. Therefore, it deals with the penalty phase of the criminal process for admitted offenders not the fact-finding phase. Daly's (2003) work differs greatly from Braithwaite (1989) largely due to the fact that she deals with myths of restorative justice and furthermore she uses data obtained from observing conferences to achieve her objective. She discovered that participants engaged in a flexible incorporation of multiple justice aims which included some elements of retributive justice, censure for past offences, some elements of rehabilitative justice in the form of asking questions such as what could be done to encourage future law abiding behaviour and some elements of restorative justice such as how the offender might make up for what they had done to the victim (Daly citied in Johnstone et al., 2003).

As a result of her findings, Daly (2003) was provoked to consider the relationship between restorative and retributive justice and the role of punishment in restorative justice. She states that because the terms 'retributive justice' and 'restorative justice' have such strong meanings and are largely used by advocates as metaphors for the bad and the good justice, perhaps they should be analysed in a way that explains current and future justice practices (Daly citied in Johnstone et al., 2003). Daly does not concur that the practices of restorative justice, which are in operation in some jurisdictions are replicas of pre-modern forms of justice, rather they are new justice practices, which have many bits of 'old' in them. By the old justice, Daly refers to modern practices of courthouse justice which permit no interaction between victim and offender, where legal actors and other experts do the talking and make decisions and whose stated aim is to punish or, at times, reform an offender. By the new justice, she refers to a variety of recent practices which bring victims and offenders, as well as others, together in a process where both lay and legal actors make decisions and whose aim is to repair harm for victims, offenders and other members of the 'community' in ways that matter to them. Therefore, as Braithwaite and Petit contend, restorative justice has a better chance than 'just deserts' of being made equally available to both rich and poor (Braitwaite & Petit, 1990).

In the alienated urban context where the existence of an ethnic community is not always recognised in a satisfactory way, a criminal justice system aimed at restoration can construct a community of care around a specific victim or offender from diverse backgrounds. It is a form of social and cultural empowerment, which permits a wider process of social control (Daly and Braithwaite citied in Johnstone et al., 2003). Braithwaite (1989) further states that restorative justice must be a culturally diverse social movement that accommodates a rich plurality of strategies in pursuit of the truths it holds to be universal. We can achieve this, he believes, by carrying out a culturally specific investigation into how to save and revive restorative justice practices that remain in all societies and how to transform state criminal justice by making it both more restorative and by rendering its abuses of power more vulnerable to restorative justice. Daly agrees with Braithwaite's ideal of a culturally diverse social movement, and states that the real story of restorative justice offers hope, not only for a better way to do justice, but also for the strengthening of mechanisms of informal social control and as a means of minimising reliance on formal aspects of social control, primarily the machinery and institutions of criminal justice. This approach was used with success in the resolution of the sectarian conflict in Northern Ireland.

USING 'AFFECT THEORY' IN RESTORATIVE PRACTICES FOR DIVERSE GROUPS

Whilst Braithwaite's theory of 'reintegrative shaming' has been to the fore within the field of restorative justice, Sylvan Tomkins' (1962) theory provides a greater understanding of the benefits of the restorative conferencing process for diverse groups. Tomkins' *Affect Theory* is based on a psychological theory of human affect. The term 'Affect' which Tomkins uses specifically refers to the biological portion of emotion or, what he calls, 'the hard-wired, pre-programmed, genetically transmitted mechanisms' that are present in each human being. These mechanisms, when triggered, precipitate a known pattern of biological events. However, it is also acknowledged that, in adults, the affective experience is a result of both the innate mechanism and a complex system of nested and interacting ideo-affective formations. Tomkins theory has been analysed and presented in more detail through the work of Nathanson (1992). Affect theory is a very effective tool in explaining the success of the scripted conference. The conferencing process encourages free expression of affect, which is the biological basis for emotion and feeling. The conference provides an opportunity for participants to express true feelings while minimising negative affects and maximising positive affects. According to Tomkins' theory this kind of environment is the ideal setting for healthy human relationships, and may have a positive impact in a multicultural setting. This approach may help to reduce the intensity of the affects, and may be applied with relevant cultural sensitivity (Leonard & Kenny, 2010).

Conferencing may also reduce ethnic tensions. When the conference reaches the agreement phase, participants are usually able to express positive thoughts. This is particularly evident when participants are asked to respond to the following scripted questions, 'What do you think/feel about what has been said?' 'What do you think about what has happened here?' 'What would you like to come out of the meeting?' People recognise the impact seen on others' faces and tend to respond to the same affect. When one is angry, others become angry. When one feels better and smiles, so do others. Tomkins refers to this as 'affective resonance' or empathy. Through this 'affective resonance' conference participants make the emotional journey together feeling each other's feelings as they move from anger, distress and shame to interest and enjoyment. For the conference, the prospective facilitator can take comfort and gain confidence in understanding that Tomkins (1962) 'Affect theory' is reliably demonstrated by the scripted conference process. Participants consistently move from negative to positive feelings in the safe and structured environment created by the script (O'Connell, Wachtel, & Wachtel, 1999).

Nathanson's (1992) 'compass of shame' makes it very clear how people from diverse backgrounds react to each other and express their shame. Nathanson argues that people usually react with one or more of four general patterns or 'scripts' which he depicts as directions on a compass: attack other, attack self, withdrawal and avoidance. For example, when parents of offending children blame and criticise the school or the police officer when confronted with an offence, they demonstrate the *attack other* response. These parents of offenders try to avoid shame by putting the responsibility on others. This is a common response to shame demonstrated in today's society. Another contemporary response is avoidance through alcohol, drug abuse or thrill-seeking behaviour such as joy riding. Several decades ago the common responses to shame were *attack self* and *withdrawal*. In *attack self* the shamed individuals are self-punishing and unreasonably hard on themselves. In withdrawal, the shamed individuals hide as a result of being overwhelmed by the shame (Leonard & Kenny, 2010).

While these responses to shame are normal, they are harmful and need to be addressed (O'Connell et al., 1999). Conferences can help people move beyond the compass of shame through acknowledgement and expression of shame and through subsequent reintegration. Due to the fact that the restorative conference affirms the intrinsic worth of the wrongdoer and condemns only the objectionable behaviour, parents and offenders feel less threatened and more equipped to acknowledge responsibility. O'Connell et al. (1999) further argues, along with other theorists such as Braithwaite (1989) and Daly (2003), that victims also experience shame. Victims may blame themselves for the incident, withdraw and hide their feelings and sometimes distract themselves. Victims may also 'lash out' at others close to them who are not responsible for the offence. In providing an outlet for expressing feelings and moving beyond shame to resolution, restitution and reintegration, the restorative conference is as important to victims as it is to offenders (O'Connell et al., 1999). This process paves the way for improved cultural understandings in place of mistrust and misunderstandings from poorly informed cultural assumptions.

CONCLUSION

As this chapter has demonstrated, Ireland has a long way to go to meet the issues of diversity, multiculturalism, social justice and racism head on, in order to stop any increase in racist behaviour amounts its public. This chapter has outlined the benefits of promoting evidence-based training in the area of practitioner's engagement with diverse groups in society. In so doing, sensitively trained and qualified instructors can prepare the ground for a more inclusive society. The chapter examined the importance of culturally sensitive instruction of frontline practitioners. In addition, it examined the training of facilitators within the context of restorative justice practice. It argues that Tomkins may seek to look beyond understandings of 'culture as identity' to develop his themes of 'Affect' in society, with the result that sometimes locally produced and state supported initiatives may emerge from these processes. Tomkins refers to this as 'affective resonance' or empathy. Through this 'affective resonance' conference practitioners and citizens make the emotional journey together, understanding each other's perspective as they move towards a multicultural perspective.

Whether in the context of inter-culturalism or multiculturalism, preparing practitioners and volunteers for conflict resolution between individuals or groups of various ethnic backgrounds creates better outcomes within the justice system. This, in turn, builds confidence across diverse groups within the justice system and wider processes of the state. Ultimately, a better citizenry is developed, built on a shared sense of mutual purpose, with increased understanding and tolerance emerging as a result. With properly trained practitioners and volunteers, shared understandings can be developed from ethnic conflict and misunderstanding.

NOTES

1. Baker, Lynch, Cantillon and Walsh's *Equality: From Theory to Practice* (2004) outlines the role of the state's legal framework in positively highlighting (or sometimes negatively reinforcing) inequality in society.
2. Flaherty (2016).
3. According to Consedine (1995) the restorative approach to crime came about following mounting concern over the exclusion of the victim from the criminal justice system and also through the belief that there was a lack of participation by the offender. He believes that the restorative justice process recognises a worldview that says we are all interconnected and that what we do, be it for good or evil, has an impact on others.
4. National Drugs Strategy, 2001–2008, O'Connell (1998), Fountain (2006), Corr (2004), D'Avanzo, Frye, and Forman (1994), and Sangster, Shiner, Patel and Sheikh (2002) are all cited from The National Advisory Committee on Drugs (NACD), submission to the Health Service Executive's (HSE) *National Intercultural Strategy*, 2007.
5. Fountain (2004). Greater London Authority, cf. The National Advisory Committee on Drugs (NACD) 2007.
6. Other barriers to effective dealings with minorities in the area of drug abuse set out by NACD (2007) include 'lack of awareness and denial of drug use due to cultural stigmas, and a lack of knowledge and relevant training in the area of drug abuse amongst minorities' NACD (2007).
7. For Braithwaite, reintegrative shaming prevents crime, while stigmatisation is a form of shaming which makes crime problems worse.

REFERENCES

Aerston, I. (2000). *Offender mediation in Europe: Making restorative justice work*. Leuven: Leuven University Press.

Baker, J., Lynch, K., Cantillon, S., & Walsh, J. (2004). *Equality: From theory to action*. Basingstoke: Palgrave MacMillan.

Braithwaite, J. (1989). *Crime, shame and reintegration*. Cambridge: Cambridge University Press.

Braithwaite, J. (2003). Restorative justice and a better future' cited. In G. Johnstone (Eds.), *A restorative justice reader: Texts, sources, context*. Devon: Willan Publishing.

Braithwaite, J., & Pettit, P. (1990). *Not just desserts: A republican theory of criminal justice* (4th ed.). Oxford: Oxford University Press.

Consedine, J. (1995). *Restorative justice: Healing the effects of crime*. Lyttelon: Ploughshares Publications.

Corr, C. (2004). *Drug use among new communities in Ireland: An exploratory study*. Merchant's Quay Ireland, NACD, Dublin.

Daly, K. (2003). Mind the gap: Restorative justice in theory and practice. In A. von Hirsch, J. Roberts, A. E. Bottoms, K. Roach, & M. Schiff (Eds.). *Restorative justice and criminal justice: Competing or reconcilable paradigms?* (pp. 219–236). Oxford. Hart Publishing.

D'Avanzo, C., Frye, B., & Forman, R. (1994). Culture, stress and substance use in Cambodia refugee women. *Journal of Studies on Alcohol*, *55*(4), 420–426.

Flaherty, R. (2016). *Ireland sees record number of racist assaults in 2015* – report. *Irish Times*, August 2, 2016.

Fountain, J. (Ed.). (2004). *Young refugees and asylum seekers in greater London: Vulnerability to problematic drug use*. London: Greater London Authority.

Fountain, J. (2006). *An overview of the nature and extent of illicit drug use among the traveller community: An exploratory study*. Centre for Ethnicity and Health, University of Central Lancashire, Preston.

Government of Ireland. (2005). *National Action Plan against Racism (NPAR): Planning for diversity*. Dublin: Government Press Office.

Holland, K. (2016). State violating traveller's human rights, council finds. *Irish Times*, May 16, 2016.

Leonard, L., & Kenny, P. (2010). Preparing for equality and training for diversity within the criminal justice system in the republic of Ireland. *Translocations: Migration and Social Change Journal*, January 10, 2010.

Maguire, M., & Titley, G. (2010). Introduction to special edition on integration. *Translocations: Migration and Social Change Journal*, January 10, 2010.

Nathanson, D. (1992). *Shame & pride: Affect, sex & the birth of the self*. New York, NY: Norton & Company.

National Advisory Committee on Drugs (NACD). (2007). *Submission to the health service executive's national intercultural strategy*. Dublin: NACD.

National Drugs Strategy. (2001–2008). *Building on experience*. Dublin: Department of Tourism, Sport and Recreation, Stationary Office.

O'Connell, J. (1998). *Travellers in Ireland: An examination of discrimination and racism*. www.paveepoint.ie/pav_ireac.html

O'Connell, T., Wachtel, T., & Wachtel, B. (1999). *REAL justice conferencing handbook*. Pennsylvania, PA: The Piper's Press.

O'Mahony, P. (2001). *Prison policy in Ireland*. Cork: Cork University Press.

Sangster, D., Shiner, M., Patel, K., & Sheikh, N. (2002). *Delivering drug services to Black and ethnic minority communities*. DPAS Paper 16: Public Policy Research Unit, Goldsmith College, University of London and Ethnicity and Health Unit, University of Central Lancashire.

Tomkins, S. S. (1962). *Affect imagery consciousness: The positive affects*. (Vol. 1). New York, NY: Springer.

Tonry, M. (Eds.). (1998). *The handbook of crime and punishment*. New York, NY: Oxford University Press.

Van Ness, D., & Strong, K. (1997). *Restoring justice*. Cincinnati, OH: Anderson.

CHAPTER 9

RESTORATIVE JUSTICE

ABSTRACT

The chapter will examine the emergence and influence of the restorative justice movement as a bridge between communities, civil society and the state in Ireland. The chapter will focus on the Republic of Ireland, but will also examine restorative conferencing in Northern Ireland. This will be divided into a number of sections, each reflecting the emergence of a movement dedicated to the promotion of restorative justice as a vehicle for a holistic form of community-based justice in Ireland. This chapter covers the history, scope, and philosophical-political background of the restorative justice movement, providing specific examples of the interchange between this restorative justice movement and civil society in Ireland, Northern Ireland and the United States. The wider potential of the restorative justice movement will be highlighted.

This potential is demonstrated in the restorative movement's challenge to understandings of failed punitive approaches, and through its socially redemptive alternative which emphasises collective responsibility for crime amongst all of the community. The chapter will also examine the international background to restorative justice, and its theoretical understandings, with a focus on key theorists such as Strang and Braithwaite, amongst others. It will examine salient issues that underpin social justice and social control in Ireland, including the potential impacts of restorative justice policy and practice for the wider community and the state.

Keywords: Restorative justice; civil society; social movements; state; community; conference

> Restorative justice has become the slogan of a global social movement ... and a profoundly influential social movement throughout the world
>
> – Braithwaite (1996, pp. 23–24)

INTRODUCTION

The literature on social movements and civil society in Ireland has produced little analysis of the links between communities, civil society and the state in the area of justice. This chapter will address that gap, bridging in the process what has been described as 'two of the "hottest" but inchoate topics in social sciences-civil society and restorative justice' (Strang & Braithwaite, 2001, p. 1). Moreover, the pursuit of forms of restored justice by a civil society was at the heart of Enlightenment thinking, and remains central to the rights-based societies of the contemporary era. In order to develop understandings of these themes further, the chapter will outline the processes of restorative justice practice within the context of Irish civil society, itself a 'contested' field, according to Geoghegan and Powell (in Ó Broin & Kirby, 2009, p. 95).

One of the key issues at the heart of this debate is the acceptance of 'justice' as a salient issue within the rubric of 'community', whether it is in the context of development or cultural expression. Furthermore, as Geoghegan and Powell and also Kieran Allen (2000, 2007) have argued, any debate about justice in the community must first acknowledge the impact of social inequality on all levels of Irish society in recent years. For Allen, the networks of power which underpin levels of privilege and inequality in society pervade all levels of life in contemporary Ireland, and create a justice dichotomy for many left 'outside the tent' of such power elites. This body of criticism has tended to incorporate a critique of 'social partnership' as a contributory element to societal inequity and injustice. Nonetheless, this chapter will highlight both the benefits and difficulties which emerge from a partnership approach to restorative justice policy and practice in the Irish case.

CIVIL SOCIETY AND RESTORATIVE JUSTICE

In the main, the relationship between civil society and justice in Ireland can be seen as one which has been embedded in a community-oriented move towards restoration, as opposed to the legal system's overriding concern for retribution. We can locate this process of community healing within the bounds of civil society by establishing which networks are working in the field and by identifying the outcomes of the interactions between civil society groups and the agencies of the state. Further understandings of the social, cultural and legal outcomes of the mobilisation of the various elements of the restorative justice movement in Ireland can then be established. As stated earlier, the conceptualisation of 'civil society' is itself contested. Therefore, the four contemporary understandings of 'civil society' set out by Scholte (2007, p. 16) will be applied to the Irish restorative justice movement here. These understandings, which are congruent with the key principles of restorative practices, include:

i. the 'quality of human collectivity', based on tolerance, trust and non-violence;
ii. a 'political space, an arena where citizens congregate to deliberate';
iii. the 'sum total of associational life within a given human collectivity';
iv. 'third sector non-governmental organisations (NGOs)' (Scholte, 2007, p. 16).

BACKGROUND

The restorative element in Irish understandings of the relationship between justice and civil society can be traced back through history. Early Celtic law contained elements of social restoration. The following quote from the eminent Gaelic scholar Eoin MacNeill sets out an understanding of the communal and restorative elements contained in early Celtic Law:

> We have evidence that Irish Law worked well, that it produced among the common people a feeling of satisfaction with its operation and with its measure of justice and peace it brought into their lives. (MacNeill, 1935, p. 151)

Brehon Law also contained a balance between the sometime competing aims of 'law' and 'justice', for both victim and offender, in the areas of compensation and redress, which could be negotiated. According to the ancient law text *An Críth Gablach*, laws could be interpreted according to the understanding of the crime and the rank of those involved, such as royalty, craftsmen and the *fílí* or court poets. This represented the initial involvement of the wider population in law in ancient Ireland, which recognised up to seven ranks within its civil society, distinguishing Brehon Law from its more rigid Saxon counterpart (ibid). By the 1600s, the Confederation of Kilkenny social movement rebelled against the unfair statutes imposed by the parliament. Daniel O'Connell's Repeal movement was a rights-based mobilisation in pursuit of justice for the Catholic population in the 1800s.

This relationship between justice and civil society continued into the twentieth century. The Sinn Fein courts would go on to revive the concept of community justice during the War of Independence. Justice-based movements have mobilised in pursuit of social change throughout Ireland's recent past, including the trade union movement, the civil rights movement in Northern Ireland, the women's movement, the environmental movement and the alter-globalisation movement (Allen, 2007; Connolly, 2002, 2003; Connolly & Hourigan, 2006; Cox, 2006; Leonard, 2006, 2008). In recent decades, paramilitaries and vigilante groups have presented a darker form of community justice. In many of these cases, a form of community restoration has been undertaken in the aftermath of periods of intolerance or inequality (Tomlinson, Varley, & McCullagh, 1988). The following section will examine the theoretical concepts which underpin the formation of restorative justice movements in society.

THEORY

Restorative Justice is a distinct philosophy of justice, which focuses on making amends for harm done (Edgar & Newell, 2006; Wright, 1999). Essentially, restorative justice fulfils the basic requirements of the 'social contract' which in the philosophies of Hobbes and Rousseau forms the basis of civil society. The fundamental principle of restorative philosophy is that when a person has harmed another, the most useful response is to try to repair the harm (Consedine, 1995; Johnstone & Van Ness, 2007). Restorative justice stretches far beyond ideas about criminal justice to encompass civil renewal, individual responsibility, conflict resolution, empowerment, shaming and forgiveness (Braithwaite, 1998; Hudson, 2003). Whilst the term 'restorative justice' in itself is relatively recent, when reviewed in the context of its historical development it becomes apparent that key terms of restitution, reparation, compensation, reconciliation, atonement, redress, community service, mediation are all used interchangeably in the literature (Weitekamp & Kerner, 2002). These key terms have collectively been united under the umbrella of what is now known as restorative justice.

Restorative justice operates within and outside of the criminal justice process, through policy initiatives and civil society responses (McCold, 2004; Morris & Maxwell, 2002). Whilst it may have only come to prominence in Western societies in the 1980s, the concept is far from new and can be linked to traditions of the Celts, Maori, Samoans, other indigenous peoples, as well as having roots in various religious communities (Consedine, 1995; Gelsthorpe & Morris, 2002). For some commentators it is not a new form of justice but rather dates back and returns society to pre modern forms of justice (Zehr, 1990). In this context restorative justice is seen as timeless, with the modern criminal justice system as an abnormal development requiring explanation (Crawford & Newburn, 2002; Daly, 2002). The modern state is considered to have 'stolen the conflict' from communities, victims and offenders, and in the process buried long-standing traditions of restorative justice (Christie, 1977). Some go as far to suggest that restorative justice has been the dominant model of criminal justice throughout most of human history for all of the world's people (Braithwaite, 1998). Furthermore, its re-emergence in recent decades is connected to a number of social, political and cultural changes, for example the re-articulation of rights and responsibilities between the state and civil society particularly inspired by neo-liberal assaults on the welfare state, and the increasing salience given to victims of crime (Crawford & Newburn, 2002).

PRACTICE

The practical aim of restorative justice is to consider the impact on victims and others involved, be they family, friends, peers or members of the wider community (Sharpe, 1998). It also endeavours to explore the impact upon the community and implicitly seeks to limit the role of legal professionals. Advocating Christie's call 'let's have as few experts as we dare' (1977, p. 12), restorative justice prefers to empower victims, offenders, family members and others as partners in the justice process. According to Crawford and Newburn (2002,

p. 22): 'these are the new stakeholders of a revised vision of justice, which seeks to recognise and bring into play, through their active involvement, a broader conceptualisation of the appropriate key actors in dispute processing and resolution'. Therefore restorative justice relocates authority in responses to crime away from the state to stakeholders themselves who are afforded the maximum degree of control over deliberation and decision-making (Hudson, 2003). In the case of the Republic of Ireland the relocation of authority from the state to the community is an issue.

Secondly, the importance of participatory and deliberative processes emphasises the value of participation, empowerment, communication, dialogue and negotiated agreements. Informal environments in which stakeholders are comfortable are conducive to good communication between parties. At the heart of the restorative justice philosophy lies a concern with a particular mode of participatory conflict resolution that centres on consensus building through a problem solving approach to crime that is grounded in local knowledge and local capacity (Johnstone & Van Ness, 2007). Restorative processes emphasise the importance of offender and victim participation – choice and control in the process of face-to-face encounters and decision-making. Restoring a sense of control to the central parties is a key aspect of the restorative process (Wright, 1999). One intended consequence of party-centred control and participation is to restore responsibility to participants, in the belief that this will encourage offenders to be more accountable for their actions and to encourage others to take responsibility for ensuring the successful implementation of any agreement reached (Morris & Maxwell, 2002).

Discussing the consequences of offences is seen to be a more powerful way of communicating the gravity of their offence to offenders in a way that brings home the impact on victims (Morris, 2002). It is believed that a process that treats people with respect and encourages their empowerment is more legitimate in the eyes of those participating. Furthermore that it encourages a general respect for the law and understanding of the consequences of individual action on others (McCold, 2001). Irish community-based restorative justice programmes encourage participation, empowerment, communication, dialogue and negotiated agreements between parties. Thirdly, restorative justice maintains and appeals to particular restorative outcomes or resolutions. Repairing the harm caused by the crime to all of those directly and indirectly affected is the ultimate aim of restorative interventions. Reparation may be symbolic as well as material, the intention being that outcomes should seek to heal relationships (Braithwaite, 1998). In practice, these often include verbal or written apologies, compensation or direct reparation to the victim for the harm and indirect reparation to the community, which may take a variety of forms (Hudson, 2003). It is suggested that restorative outcomes should be flexible and party-centred as well as problem-oriented (Johnstone, 2002). The outcomes of restorative justice processes will be a key area of research analysis in the context of the Republic of Ireland.

Restorative practices have been expanding over the past 30 years, and as a result a range of approaches have been applied to different problems including family relationships, school bullying, training programmes, industrial relations and complaints against police in addition to all types of crime. However the range of practices and programmes of restorative justice are too diverse for there to be an agreed definition (Daly, 2002). Whilst some place emphasise on core values and principles, others focus on aims and outcomes or make reference to specific programmes or practices (Hoyle & Young, 2002; Hudson, 2003). Despite this difficulty it's widely accepted that restorative justice is a face-to-face process that involves offenders, victims, their representatives and representatives of the community coming together to agree a response to a crime (Bazemore & Walgrave, 1999; Braithwaite, 1998; Zehr, 1990).

CIVIL SOCIETY

The Irish version of the restorative justice movement has its roots in the international movements which have shaped understandings of restorative justice for over 30 years. The inception of the modern restorative justice movement can be found within the civil rights and women's movements of the 1960s. The U.S. civil rights movement was, in their view, partially rooted in critiques of institutional racism in the American justice system. This racial critique also framed their arguments around the disproportionate imprisonment of African-Americans and other minority groups, such as Native Americans. Campaigns for prisoners' rights and alternatives to imprisonment can also be traced back to the 'new left' era. In the United States, in addition, challenges to unfair justice systems occurred in other jurisdictions, including Australia, Canada, New Zealand and South Africa. The women's movement also provided an important focus on crimes of violence against women, which argued for better alternatives in justice. According to Daly and Immarigeon (ibid) 'feminist organising, and feminist groups were among the first to call attention to the mistreatment of victims in the criminal justice process' and prisoners' rights campaigns. These early advocates in the restorative justice movement mobilised around problems for society emanating from an over-reliance on prisons alongside the lack of a voice for victims in the justice process.

Daly and Immarigeon (*ibid.*) also outline the various kinds of initiatives which gave rise to the wider mobilisation of the restorative justice movement. These included the following initiatives which empowered victims and communities including: Prisoner Rights and Alternatives to Prisons; Conflict Resolution; Victim-Offender Reconciliation Programs (VORPs); Victim-Offender Mediation (VOMs); Victim Advocacy; Family Group Conferences/ the 'Wagga' Model (FGCs); Sentencing Circles; Victim Impact Panels (originally established by Mothers against Drunk Driving or MADD) (*ibid.*). As with many of the new left movement that emerged from the counterculture, research and academic inquiry into justice alternatives ran in parallel (or followed local initiatives) with social movement activism in the pursuit of alternatives to existing justice system practices was academic research and theories, including the following:

CIVIL SOCIETY IN IRELAND

In order to better understand the potential of civil society as an element of the criminal justice system through the activities of the restorative justice movement, we must first outline the basis of civil society as it operates in Ireland. Civil society as a sector in Irish society includes a diverse range of actors ranging from trade unions, local development agencies, business interests, advocates and academics, media interests, and the various strata of local and national government who create improved conditions or provide funding for most agencies active in the sector. In addition, the civil society sector incorporates a range of rights-based non-governmental organisations (NGOs) and social movements, including social justice groups, women's rights groups and ethnic and equality advocates. All of these work within the context of an engaged civil society sector that had been given some access to power throughout the years of neo-corporatist social partnership.

This access in turn created some leverage for those stakeholders who were denied a place at the partnership table that in time came to be dominated by the key players in the development of economic growth represented by the state, unions and business lobby (Doran, 2008; Leonard, 2008). One offshoot of this emphasis on growth creation was the creation of a 'two-tier' society with a dichotomy between economic players and those who worked to highlight non-economic issues. Therefore, it must be recognised that those advocating for restorative justice had to operate within this dichotomous socio-political culture. Nonetheless, as players within the realm of civil society, those advocating for restorative justice have had some degree of success through the introduction of the concept as an aspect of justice policy in Ireland at both the institutional and community levels.

Northern Ireland's civil society sector has been traditionally bound up with the local operations of the British welfare state.[1] However, the peace process has given some impetus to a justice-based civil society in the North. The debate about communities and justice in Northern Ireland has been a long-standing feature of the process of reconciliation in that jurisdiction. Throughout the decades of the 'Troubles', communities have been characterised by religious or political affiliations; Catholic/Nationalist or Protestant/Loyalist. Justice within these communities was a most troubled concept, and grassroots justice and local control initiatives included punishment beatings, kneecappings and vigilante groups. Despite the onset of the Peace-Process following the Good Friday Agreement in 1998, ownership over processes of justice remains a contested terrain in Northern Ireland (McEvoy & Eriksson, 2008, p. 157). In addition, the years of the 'Troubles' gave rise to the dominance of republican or loyalist agendas, which in turn constrained a 'natural' non-state or non-sectarian civil society emerging. Restorative justice and community conferencing holds out the possibility of a successful alternative to the traditional intransigence of the two traditions in relation to the provision of locally managed justice initiatives in the North.

Essentially, a restorative justice *movement* can be said to exist in both jurisdictions in Ireland, based on civil society groupings which are linked through various networks of civil society governance, both nationally and globally. This movement is mobilised through the four elements of civil society outlined above. Although lacking the counter-hegemonic basis of other civil society movements,[2] the restorative justice movement is in many ways representative of a radical approach to grassroots governance based on a conceptualisation of justice which is embedded in the community. Within this public space, existing notions of punitiveness are challenged in a manner which promotes collective responsibility and inclusive deliberation. The mediation processes of restorative practice can be applied to individual, group or community issues, and can be extended out to provide a wider extent of engagement by concerned parties. By providing this extensive and collective range of community-based mediation, the restorative justice movement can address the provision of justice within the parameters of local discourse and situational habitus.

The primary elements of the restorative justice movement in Ireland are, in the main, embedded in the structures of civil society. This incorporates many local and national non-governmental organisations (NGOs), agencies and community-based groups who are advocating for justice reforms. Amongst the many groups involved with restorative justice at the civil society level is the programme for *Real Justice*, the Restorative Justice Network Ireland, the Irish Penal Reform Trust (IPRT), Amnesty International's Irish section, Barnardos, the Children's Rights Alliance, the Irish Council for Civil Liberties (ICCL), amongst others. In addition, international networks are created with restorative justice advocates internationally. Agencies of the state that work in the area of restorative justice include *An Garda Síochána*, the Department of Equality and Law Reform, the Courts Services and the Human Rights Commission, the HSE Social Workers and the Probation and Welfare Service. The overlapping elements within these two aspects of third and state sector create a functioning civil society which has the potential to engender reforms in the area of justice provision in Ireland, making the restorative justice a more effective element of contemporary civil society activism. In Northern Ireland, Religious and pastoral groups have worked in restorative justice and community mediation as part of the wider mediation following on from the Peace Process.

RESTORATIVE JUSTICE IN NORTHERN IRELAND

In the aftermath of the paramilitary ceasefires, most punishment activity has been discontinued, as both communities strive to forge a sustainable peace. In the pursuit of a grassroots solution, leaders from both communities have embraced restorative principles. It was around this time that the ideas of restorative justice were being introduced to Northern Ireland and were adopted by both Republican and Loyalist communities, reflecting the desire for a community-based system of justice. In the late 1980s, restorative justice projects were set up in both communities, with funding from Chuck Feeney's Atlantic Philanthropies. These were 'Community Restorative Justice Ireland' on the Republican side, while 'Alternatives to Justice' was established by activists from the Loyalist community. The Loyalist group found success working with young people involved in anti-social activities, including in the process of victim-offender mediation, reparation to the community and educational projects, alongside local mediation of neighbourhood disputes (Gormally, 2006). The Republican-based Community Restorative Justice Ireland, are established across Northern Ireland. The project organises mediation processes involving community activists as mediators between offenders and victims, while also providing educational services. The success of these initiatives is a reflection of the positivity emerging from communities which had suffered disproportionately during the conflict. According to Gormally (2006): 'The idea of restorative justice is sweeping through the communities. The ideas of restorative justice have formed the core of what has become a real social movement'.

CIVIL SOCIETY AND THE IRISH STATE

Since the early 1990s the Irish State has been subject to repeated criticism for failing to provide adequate responses to youth offending and for being archaic and out of tune with contemporary developments in youth justice policy (O'Mahony & Deaziey, 2000; O'Sullivan, 1996; Quinn, 2002). Despite a plethora of committees and reports that set out specific recommendations for the reform of child care and youth justice policy from the 1970s onwards (*Kennedy Report*, 1970; *Task Force on Child Care Services*, 1980; *Whittaker Report*, 1985), there has been little or no response from the Irish State until relatively recently (Kilkelly, 2006; Seymour, 2004; Walsh, 2005). Unlike England and Wales, the impetus for reform only gained momentum in the mid-1990s, when a government select committee entitled 'Juvenile Crime-Its Causes and its Remedies' (1992) made specific recommendations for the development of a framework for youth justice reform. The 'Children Bill' (1996) reflects this framework and subsequent reforms to policy came to be enshrined in the Children Act 2001. It is the intention of the state that the Act, will, when fully implemented update Irish youth justice policy by replacing the Children Act 1908, and in doing so bring Ireland into line with international youth justice standards (Kilkelly, 2006; Walsh, 2005).

The framing processes of the restorative justice movement have suffered from a lack of published material. In turn, this has led to a limited debate about the key issues, influences and direction of the system; this in turn has significantly contributed to the lack of political interest and desire to reform the system (O'Donnell, 2008; Seymour, 2004). At present there is no centralised system of data collection in the area and according to Walsh (2005) it would not be an exaggeration to conclude that Irish criminal justice statistics are in a bit of a mess. Statistics available have been criticised as 'outdated, partial, limited, non-integrated and poorly explained' (O'Dwyer, 2002, p. 182). The severe absence of data not only impedes the framing agenda of third sector groups but also makes the development and implementation of policy extremely and unnecessarily arduous. The lack of available research has resulted in any policy being developed in a 'research vacuum' (O'Sullivan, 1996, p. 5) At present the only data available on youth offending patterns and behaviour is complied by *An Garda Síochána* which in itself is problematic, as it does not provide a detailed breakdown of the total number of convictions or the demographics of youth offenders. Data on prisons and places of detention is inconsistent and ceases to exist after 1994 (Walsh, 2005).

YOUTH JUSTICE

Lobbying by third sector groups led to Ireland ratifying the United Nations *Convention on the Rights of the Child* in 1992. The Irish state was later criticised by the UN committee, who expressed concern regarding the treatment of children deprived of their liberty in light of the principles of the UN Convention and other international standards (Children's Rights Alliance, 1998).[3] This international pressure coupled with calls from independent and non-statutory organisations, lobby groups and members of the academic community played a major role in forcing the state to take action and deal with decades of youth justice neglect. Furthermore in a country the size of Ireland (4.2 million, *Central Statistics Office Ireland*, 2006) extensive media reporting and coverage of certain isolated, but serious events involving youthful offending, often serve to swing the political pendulum towards reactionary punitiveness rather than strategic crime prevention in order to calm public concern about crime (Seymour, 2004).[4]

Over the past decade there has been a significant change in third sector focus, which has gradually shifted towards considering children's rights, with developments in the *National Children's Strategy* (2000), the creation of a Junior Ministry with special responsibility for children (2002), the appointment of an Ombudsman for Children (2003) and the establishment of National

Children's Office (2005). The ministry uniquely encompasses the Departments of Health, Education and Justice and has enabled/necessitated inter departmental co-operation. These incentives have served to elevate the status and profile of preventative work with children and their families and are hoped to augment the possibilities for positive developments for the future (Quinn, 2002).

However, whilst recent developments in the area of youth justice are encouraging and long overdue, there still are major gaps in the programme for reform. Seven years on from *The Children Act* (2001), its content has only partly been enacted. Change at governmental level and the establishment of a designated Youth Justice Service (YJS) in 2006 has done little to improve the plight of children and young people in conflict with the law. The service is intended to bring together services for young offenders under one, governance and management structure. The review (which received submissions from a wide spectrum) was the first extensive official enquiry into the operation of the youth justice system in Ireland. Whilst it was noted by the committee that it would sit most comfortably within a care and social services environment, reflecting practice in other countries, the fact that no existing social service structure seems appropriate for the incorporation of a youth care and justice service at this time, persuaded it to recommend placing the body as an executive office of the Department of Justice, Equality and Law Reform on an interim basis. The objectives of the office, whose position is to be reviewed in five years, include the development of a single unified youth justice policy, implementation of youth justice strategies, assumption of responsibility for detention orders for all offenders under 18 years of age; implementation of the provisions of the Children Act 2001 in relation to community sanctions, restorative justice conferencing and diversion and finally co-ordination of service delivery at national and local level.

The Children Act (2001) advocates a strong restorative approach to all aspects of dealing with youth crime and the fact that it is being introduced on a gradual basis by the state puts the system in an unnecessary transitory process. In recent years the media and as a direct result political attention has focused on the level of youth crime in Ireland serving to inform the public on the social problems caused by delinquency and youth crime. Civil society based restorative justice initiatives processes have been developed by third sector groups alongside *An Garda Síochána*, the Probation and Welfare Service, the Offender Reparation Programme, the Victim-Offender Mediation and the Community Based Restorative Schemes.[5]

BENEFITS AND LIMITS

The benefits for victims and offenders who engage in restorative justice processes may out weight those offered by more traditional methods, by providing a shared or community-based platform for dealing with crime and its private and public outcomes such as pain, remorse and guilt. Firstly, victims are given the opportunity to meet the offender and relate to him or her of their version of events and how the offence has affected them. Meeting with the offender also gives the victim the opportunity to understand the reason for the offence and perhaps realise that they were not singled out. The meeting may also empower them to overcome worries about possible re-victimisation. Research has shown victims are empowered through restorative justice and are satisfied by receiving an apology, reparation for the harm caused and an assurance that there will not be a reoccurrence. The community, who can be said to have failed the offender as much as the victim from a Durkheimian or 'anomic' perspective, can also partake in a community based restoration process.

Restorative conferences provide the offender with the opportunity to take responsibility and account for the actions. The restorative approach empowers them to express genuine remorse, to apologise directly to the victim and make some form of reparation financial or otherwise. It further empowers offenders to address underlying problems, which they may be having, and provides them with the opportunity to work with their parents and authorities to fully integrate themselves back into society. Restorative Justice may provide the Criminal Justice System with an alternative means of dealing with crime control across society, and even within a wider political context, such as post-conflict mediation. However, in Ireland it is only legal at present to deal with matters relating to juvenile crime through convening restorative events. The benefit of restorative justice for society and the criminal justice system is that it has implications for social control in the form of reducing future rates of crime. The juvenile offenders of today are the major criminals of tomorrow. For offenders, restoring a sense of security and empowerment can rebuild their confidence in finding employment, achieving educational success, sporting success and of feeling confident and secure in the future.

COMMUNITY EMPOWERMENT

The restorative justice philosophy involves all of those affected by the criminal behaviour be they victims, offenders, the families involved or the wider community all play their part in resolving the issues that flow from the offending. As Braithwaite contends, the restorative justice process empowers all parties to restore the deliberative control of justice by its citizens (Braithwaite, citied in Johnstone et al., 2003, p. 87). The remaining terms of the agreement came about as a result of dialogue, interaction and agreement between all parties. The community may acknowledge its own failings, and address the best outcome through mediation. Attempts at community mediation through conferencing have been undertaken as part of the dialogue about the Corrib pipeline in Mayo, with mixed results. However, the process can empower the community, who can present their shared grievance in a public forum to key actors from the state or multinationals. With such processes embedded in civil society, the third sector could provide a vital bridge between concerned communities and the de-legitimised state.

Wheeldon (2009) has outlined concerns about the co-optation of restorative justice movement within the wider socio-political system of justice due to the bridging role restorative justice can play through the links created between civil society and agencies of the state. However, the pitfalls of co-optation can be avoided through the development of a framework which allows the 'third sector' groups of civil society to work with the community-orientated projects of state justice agencies such as *An Garda Síochána*. Once established this creates a viable role for civil society groups within the criminal justice system, while also providing a forum for the presentation of community grievances. Essentially, the establishment of such civil society frameworks provides community activists with a degree of access to the 'political opportunity structures' of both the justice system and the wider political frameworks surrounding any dispute. The community conferencing outlined can subsequently be seen to represent a 'political mediation model' based on 'transformative mediation' (Bush & Folger, 1994).

RESTORATIVE MODELS OF COMMUNITY POLICING

Restorative Justice allows for civil society involvement and community participation in the policing of local disputes. An Garda Síochána first introduced their 'Restorative Justice Initiatives' on a pilot basis in 1999. A total of 68 events were convened between the introduction of the *Children Bill* in 1999 and the subsequent *Children Act* in 2001. Garda-based restorative conferencing operates through the Garda Juvenile Diversion Programme. The Juvenile Diversion Programme operates under the supervision and direction of the Garda Juvenile Office. The Children Act 2001 placed the Diversion Programme on a statutory footing and enshrined restorative justice into law. An Garda Síochána are the primary body for convening restorative events in Ireland, providing the force with a legitimised form of community policing, which also opens a dialogue with civil society. However, while the Gardaí are implementing restorative justice for juveniles during the present time, it is very possible that restorative justice processes could be extended to encompass adult crime and especially crime of a sensitive nature for example, sexual and child abuse cases.

The restorative justice movement provides an opportunity to achieve a fairer and more satisfactory criminal justice system for all members of society. In this way, the 'gaps' which exist in the provision of justice through civil society participation in alternative forms of policing through conferencing is established. Restorative Justice Principles are slowly being accepted as alternatives to sentencing and as a community or individual mediation process in the community in a number of cases in Ireland. There is a growing acknowledgement among professionals and academics that society needs to develop other responses to crime. The Restorative Justice process has much to offer, by way of community policing initiatives as it centres on the greater use of non-custodial sentences will bring about changes not only in the community's relationship with the law but will have significant implications for improved and deeper methods of providing social justice.

These restorative measures improve the context of policing and crime prevention in the community and enhance the processes of justice across society. Through rehabilitation and reintegration rather than traditional punitive measures offenders come to realise that there is nothing to be gained from leading a life or crime. Ultimately, as an alternative system of policing the community, restorative justice provides a significant alternative based on concepts of sustainable justice rather than short-term punitiveness:

> History is teaching us every day that if we continue to operate a criminal justice system oriented principally towards punishment based on vengeance, and continue to reap its bitter harvest of high crime rates, fear and insecurity. The time for change is now if we are to bequeath the 21st century a criminal justice system worthy of its name. (Consedine, 1995, p. 196)

CONCLUSION

The restorative justice movement in Ireland has been demonstrated to have an impact in the areas of community development, civil society, governmentality and policy delivery. These impacts have been demonstrated to occur on at least two levels; the first is at the level of extending the remit of the state through civil society's engagement with community policing in the form of the various conferencing initiatives outlined in this chapter. The second impact reflects a more contentious outcome. Such contention is demonstrated through the capacity of restorative justice to serve as a facilitator of community empowerment which strengthens civil society and third sector engagement, creating a form of social capital which has true implications for the establishment of a broader and more inclusive justice base across Irish society.

The mobilisation of any social movement has limited potential to secure complete social or cultural change in the area of contention chosen by its advocates as the social issue requiring attention. And so it is with the restorative justice movement in the Irish case. No movement can completely restore the losses incurred as a result of any injustice which occurs. Nonetheless, this chapter demonstrates that the restorative justice movement can contribute to an active civil society by creating the conditions whereby certain outcomes which are compatible with the movement's aims are achieved. These outcomes include the following:

- The amelioration of grief and suffering in the community.
- The creation of networks which facilitate dialogue between opposing parties.

- The strengthening of civil society through the facilitation of processes of engagement with the various elements of the justice system such as the police, courts and welfare services.
- The extension of the concept of justice beyond that of punishment, creating a deeper form of sustainable justice throughout society.
- The creation of 'sustainable justice' in society.

Moreover, the chapter demonstrates that the basic philosophies and aims of the restorative justice movement are congruent with the essential basis of civil society set out by Scholte's (2007, p. 16) civil society-orientated criteria of creating public space for discussion, tolerance, associational living, and the engagement of the third sector in civic affairs. Furthermore, the restorative justice movement can provide a bridge between civil society and the justice system through the provision of restorative conferencing in community based disputes.

According to Wheeldon (2009), 'The restorative justice project is challenged today by a desire both from within and outside the movement to more fully engage with the criminal justice system'. This chapter demonstrates that while the risks of co-option are real for the restorative justice movement, the processes of restorative justice hold out a much deeper promise of providing a real alternative to narrow punitive or the cycles of negativity that characterise many social or criminal disputes. In many ways, the restorative conferencing established by the police in both sections of this chapter provide the type of access to political opportunity structures required by both communities and the state in the pursuit of full mediation and the resolution of publicly held grievances.

The chapter establishes the degree to which restorative conferencing can provide an alternative to disputes about the provision of social justice, whether in areas such as community participation in policing and judication processes, through to the creation of a positive and neutral space for social expression and dialogue on different levels (including protests) through public conferencing. This creation of a 'political mediation model' based on 'transformative mediation' (Bush & Folger, 1994) addresses many of the points raised by McAdam, Tarrow, and Tilly (2001, pp. 139–143) about the 'possible interactions and outcomes' that emerge at the end of an episode of contention. This 'transformation' (or 'innovation' for movement theorists) addresses what Bush and Folger (1994) refer to as the 'destabilizing' of relationships through conflict, transforming relations through processes of mediation and the development of mutual understandings by all parties. The processes of transformative mediation discussed here uses the creation of dialogue (or 'the communication of claims as opposed to direct confrontation' according to McAdam, Tarrow, & Tilly, 2001, pp. 139–143) as a measure of success, rather than successful attainment of preconceived outcomes which may jeopardize the attainment of full restoration within the community.

NOTES

1. In 2006, the Northern Ireland Office adopted the United Nation's principles on restorative justice in its *Draft Protocol for Community-based Restorative Justice Schemes* (Sherman & Strang, 2007, p. 45).

2. Stenson and Lea examine the manner in which movements representing non-state governance from below work *with* and then *against* the State through different relationships in civil society:

> Civil society 'with the state' is presented as follows: 'Private welfare, private security, neighbourhood activism, voluntary associations, restorative justice, the courts, NGOs and private commercial regulation'. (Stenson & Lea, 2007, pp. 9–27)

3. For example, the United Nations Standard of the Minimum Rules for the Administration of Juvenile Justice (Beijing Rules), the United Nations Guidelines on the Prevention of Juvenile Delinquency (Riyadh Guidelines) and the United Nations Rules for the Protection of Juveniles Deprived of their Liberty.

4. In April 2002, following the death of two Gardaí as a result of an incident involving car theft and joyriding by juveniles, the Minister for Justice proposed plans for a temporary children's prison wing for 14 and 15 year olds in St Patrick's Institution. This plan would have been feasible under the 1908 Children Act but the Children Act 2001 when fully enacted prohibits the detention of children under 16 years of age in any place of detention.

5. This research included observations of five restorative conferences from the perspective of each of the state and third sector services available under the Children Act 2001, that is Children's Court, Probation & Welfare Service family conferencing, Garda formal and informal restorative cautions, Restorative Justice Services' Offender Reparation and Victim-Offender Mediation Programmes and Community based restorative conferencing.

REFERENCES

Allen, K. (2000). *The Celtic Tiger: The myth of social partnership in Ireland.* Manchester: Manchester University Press.

Allen, K. (2007). *The corporate takeover of Ireland.* Dublin: Irish Academic Press.

Bazemore, G., & Walgrave, L. (Eds.). (1999). *Restorative juvenile justice.* Monsey, NY: Criminal Justice Press.

Braithwaite, J. (1996). *Restorative justice and a better future.* Dorothy J. Killam Memorial Lecture, Dalhousie University, Halifax, Nova Scotia.

Braithwaite, J. (1998). Restorative justice. In M. Tonry (Eds.), *Handbook of crime and punishment.* New York, NY: Oxford University Press.

Bush, R. A. B., & Folger, J. P. (1994). *The promise of mediation.* San Francisco, CA: Jossey-Bass.

Christie, N. (1977). Conflicts as property. *British Journal of Criminology, 17,* 1–15.

Connolly, L. (2002). *The Irish women's movement: From revolution to devolution.* Dublin: Lilliput Press.

Connolly, L. (2003). *The Irish women's movement: From revolution to devolution.* London: Macmillan/Palgrave.

Connolly, L., & Hourigan, N. (Eds.). (2006). *Social movements and Ireland.* Manchester: Manchester University Press.

Consedine, J. (1995). *Restorative justice: Healing the effects of crime*. Lyttelon: Ploughshares Publications.

Cox, L. (2006). News from nowhere: The movement of movements in Ireland. In L. Connolly & N. Hourigan (Eds). *Social movements and Ireland*. Manchester: Manchester University Press.

Crawford, A., & Newburn, T. (2002). Recent developments in restorative justice for young people in England and Wales: Community participation and representation. *British Journal of Criminology*, *42*, 476–495.

Daly, K. (2002). Restorative justice: The real story. *Punishment and Society*, *4*(1), 55–79.

Doran, P. (2008). Absent friends of the earth: Minding the environmental gap in Ireland's social partnership. In M. Millar & M. Adshead (Eds.), *Governance and public policy in Ireland*. Dublin: Irish Academic Press.

Edgar, T., & Newell, T. (2006). *Restorative justice in prisons: A guide to making it happen*. Winchester: Waterside Press.

Gelsthorpe, L., & Morris, A. (2002). Restorative youth justice the last vestiges of welfare? In J. Muncie, G. Hughes, & E. McLaughlin (Eds.), *Youth justice critical readings*. London: Sage.

Gormally, B. (2006). Community restorative justice in Northern Ireland: An overview. *Restorative justice online*. Retrieved from http://www.restorativejustice.org/editions/2006/april06/gormallyarticle

Government of Ireland. (1970). *Reformatory and industrial schools systems report (The Kennedy Report)*. Dublin: Stationery Office.

Government of Ireland. (1980). *Task force on child care services: Final report to the minister for health*. Dublin: Stationery Office.

Government of Ireland. (1985). *Report of the committee of inquiry into the penal system. (The Whitaker Report)*. Dublin: Stationery Office.

Hoyle, C., & Young, R. (2002). Restorative justice: Assessing the prospects and pitfalls. In M. McConville & G. Wilson. (Eds.), *The handbook of the criminal justice process*. Oxford: Oxford University Press.

Hudson, B. (2003). *Understanding justice*. (2nd ed.). Maidenhead: McGraw-Hill Education Open University Press.

Johnstone, G. (2002). *Restorative justice: Ideas, values, debates*. Cullompton: Willan Publishing.

Johnstone, G., & Van Ness, D. W. (Eds.). (2007). *Handbook of restorative justice*. Devon: Willan Publishing.

Kilkelly, U. (2006). *Youth justice in Ireland: Tough lives, rough justice*. Dublin: Irish Academic Press.

Leonard, L. (2008). *The environmental movement in Ireland*. Dordrecht: Springer.

MacNeill, E. (1935). *Early Irish law and institutions*. Dublin: Burns, Oates and Washbourne.

McAdam, D., Tarrow, S., & Tilly, C. (2001). *Dynamics of contention*. Cambridge: Cambridge University Press.

McCold, P. (2001). Primary restorative justice practices. In A. Morris & G. Maxwell (Eds.), (2002) *Restorative justice for juveniles: Conferencing, mediation and circles*. Oxford: Hart Publishing.

McCold, P. (2004). What is the role of community in restorative justice theory and practice? In H. Zehr & B. Toews (Eds.), *Critical issues in restorative justice*. Monsey, NY: Criminal Justice Press; Devon: Willan Publishing.

McEvoy, K., & Eriksson, A. (2008). Who owns justice? Community, state and the Northern Ireland transition. In J. Shapland (Ed.), *Justice, community and civil society*. London: Willan Publishing.

Morris, A. (2002). Critiquing the critics: A brief response to critics of restorative justice. *British Journal of Criminology*, *42*(3), 596–615.

Morris, A., & Maxwell, G. (Eds.). (2002). *Restorative justice for juveniles: Conferencing, mediation and circles*. Oxford: Hart Publishing.

Ó Broin, D., & Kirby, P. (2009). *Power, dissent and democracy: Civil society and the state in Ireland*. Dublin: A & A Farmar.

O'Donnell, I. (2008). Stagnation and change in Irish penal policy. *The Howard Journal*, *47*(2), 121–133.

O'Dwyer, K. (2002). Juvenile crime and justice in Ireland. In N. Bala, J. Homick, H. Snyder, & J. Paetsch (Eds.), *Juvenile justice systems: An international comparison of problems and solutions* (pp. 153–187). Toronto: Thompson Educational Publishing.

O'Mahony, D., & Deaziey, R. (2000). *Juvenile crime and justice: Review of the criminal justice system in Northern Ireland.* Belfast: Northern Ireland Office.

O'Sullivan, E. (1996). Juvenile justice in the Republic of Ireland: Future priorities. *Irish Social Worker*, *14*(3/4), 4–7.

Quinn, M. (2002). Youth crime prevention. In P. O'Mahony (Ed.). *Criminal Justice in Ireland* (pp. 674–704). Dublin: Institute of Public Administration.

Seymour, M. (2004). *Juvenile justice in the Republic of Ireland.* Prepared for the Thematic Working Group on Juvenile Justice, European Society of Criminology. Retrieved from www.esc-eurocrim.org/files/juvenilejustice_in_the_republic_of_ireland.doc. Accessed on November 22, 2006.

Scholte, J. A. (2007). Global civil society-opportunity or obstacle for democracy In *global civil society: More or less democracy*. Development Dialogue No. 49, October 2007.

Sharpe, S. (1998). *Restorative justice: A vision for healing and change*. Edmonton: Edmonton Victim Offender Mediation Society.

Sherman, L. W., & Strang, H. (2007). *Restorative justice: The evidence*. London: Smith Institute.

Stenson, K., & Lea, J. (2007). Security, sovereignty and non-state govemance "from below". *Canadian Journal of Law and Society/Revue Canadienne Droit et Société*, *22*(2), 9–27.

Strang, H., & Braithwaite, J. (2001). *Restorative justice and civil society*. Cambridge: Cambridge University Press.

Tomlinson, M., Varley, T., & McCullagh, C. (1988). Whose law and order?: Aspects of crime and social control in Irish society. In *Studies in Irish Society Series*. Belfast: Sociology association of Ireland.

Walsh, D. (2005). *Juvenile justice*. Dublin: Thomson Roundhall.

Weitekamp, E. G. M., & Kerner, H. J. (Eds.). (2002). *Restorative* justice theoretical foundations. Devon: Willan Publishing.

Wheeldon, J. (2009). Finding common ground: Restorative justice and its theoretical construction(s). *Contemporary Justice Review*, *12*(1), 91–100.

Wright, M. (1999). *Restoring respect for justice*. Winchester: Waterside Press.

Zehr, H. (1990). *Changing lenses: A new focus for crime and justice*. Scottdale, PA: Herald Press.

CHAPTER 10

PRISONS

ABSTRACT

This chapter will examine the basis for the teaching of integrity-based competencies to prison officers as part of their training. This training underpins the performance of prison officers in the execution of their daily workplace duties, and forms a part of the 'Sustainable Justice' approach to rehabilitation. At the heart of this approach is a desire to understand and explain how a prison officer can be taught to go beyond what is the basic requirement in their tasks, in order to deliver the 'safe, secure and humane' service required of them in the Irish Prison Service (IPS) Mission Statement. The degree of success in achieving this form of elevated integrity within the prison can be seen to impact upon the lives of the prisoners in the officer's care, and on wider society as a whole.

This chapter will also discuss mentoring as a key form of learning within the prisons. While the world of the prison is one which is closed to many in society, the author gained insights when he worked as an 'embedded sociologist', working as the senior academic on the IPS recruit training programme for five years between 2008 and 2013 within Ireland's prison system. Here, he used his academic experience to put together an award-winning academic programme with his colleagues and senior IPS training staff. This experience provided him with valuable sociological understandings into the hidden world of the Irish prison system, as well as the officers who work behind their walls.

Keywords: Prison; officer; training; mentoring; justice; humane

> There is no power relation without the correlative constitution of a field of knowledge, nor any knowledge that does not presuppose and constitute at the same time power relations.
>
> – Michel Foucault (*Discipline and Punish: The Birth of the Prison*)

INTRODUCTION

When examining teaching and learning in the context of a prison, one has to ask the question 'why would anyone do such a job'? In addition, the question of how to teach staff to do such a difficult job with competency and integrity might also be posited. The answers might be found in explorations of the human condition. In his discussion of 'Integrity: Psychological, Moral, and Spiritual', Rhett Diessner sets out Socrates' three components of the Human psyche or soul: the logical-rational, the spirited or affective, and the desiring or willing (Diessner, 2007, p. 6).

The author also incorporates Kant's concepts from *the Critique of Judgment* of three faculties of the soul as 'knowledge, feeling and desire'. Therefore, we can begin to understand the basis of moral integrity and human competency as being derived from this subset of logic, spirit and desire or will. Such qualities are invariably drawn upon when humans are faced with challenges to their character, and this can be borne out by the learning experiences of prison officers who are charged with maintaining the ethos of the Irish Prison Service (IPS) Mission Statement's call for 'safe, secure and humane' approached to prison work. In particular, prison officers provide us with a good example of a group who must maintain integrity in the face of negative resistance (and on occasion, violence).

This chapter focuses on the teaching and learning processes which develop a moral and competency-based framework for prison staff. The public perception of the prison officer is often surrounded in negativity, which adds to the difficulties in developing and maintaining moral integrity for recruits to the service, within a teaching and learning environment. From the perspective of the author, understandings of these challenges and the manner in such a programme would be delivered stems from experiences working with IPS recruits as part of their academic programme, which included Sociology, Criminology and Human Rights. Throughout this process, I was able to discuss these issues with recruits, and chart their progress over a year in the prisons during participation in workplace inspections within the prisons where they worked.

One key issue which emerged from this process was an understanding of how difficult it was for recruit prison officers to come to terms with the dualistic demands they faced from internal as well as external concerns about integrity and competencies. Carl Rodgers (1961) as outlined the basis for understanding 'authentic' forms of integrity as those which are derived from inward reflection and [re]-evaluation of our personal values. For the prison officer, this process incorporates what Goffman has described as a 'dramaturgical' process; the officer must develop a 'mask' for inside and outside of work in the prison. Crawley (2004) has developed this concept further to incorporate the 'front and back' stage performances which a prison officer must act out when they are involved in different aspects in their work. For instance, they may act and say things in the officer's canteen which they then will do differently during an incident on the prison landing.

TEACHING MENTORING AS A LEARNED COMPETENCY

Officers described different types of response to this ongoing challenge to their moral integrity when faced with this challenge. Mentoring, although an unofficial part of the IPS culture (Leonard, Kenny, & McGuckin, 2009), also plays a role in the development of workplace integrity for prison officers. Recruit officers own moral understanding of their capacities at work are shaped by this unofficial mentoring process, which incorporates 'pro' and 'anti' social modelling (Cherry, 2004). Recruits must develop and maintain their own moral compass in the face of this overlapping process of negative and positive socialisation into workplace practices and dealings with the prison population. Crucially, the recruit must achieve this while both learning his trade in the prison while also dealing with sporadic episodes of violence on the landing or in the exercise yard (Edgar, O'Donnell, & Martin, 2004).

According to one study on the teaching requirements of the Irish Prison Service, Howe (2012) outlines the perception that recruits were confused about their roles. The basis of this confusion was a lack of clarity about how rehabilitation could be achieved, and how recruits could contribute to that process. From its creation in 2006, the IPS pushed to implement a process of professionalisation, with competency training at its core. From 2007, a programme of training for IPS recruits commenced, which was co-devised and co-delivered by IPS training officers and academics that were brought in from the university and Institute of Technology sectors.

The Whitaker Report of 1985 put forward a set of recommendations on the management and staffing of prisons in Ireland. In relation to the professionalisation of prison staff, Whitaker outlined the need for prison officers to move away from conflict with prisoners, in order to establish a humane regime of incarceration nationally. This theme was also highlighted in subsequent literature on prisons from the United Kingdom, with an emphasis on the need for specialised training and the establishment of pro-social competencies (Bennet, Crewe, & Waihidin, 2007; Coyle, 2005; Crawley, 2004; Liebling, 2011; Liebling, Price, & Shefer, 2011). Howe (2012) also establishes an understanding of the significance played by the prevailing atmosphere in each prison in the development of learning patterns for recruits, a point which must be acknowledged by anyone teaching prison staff. Recruits learn by interaction on the job in attrition to any teaching provided externally, and relevant teaching programmes must include prior knowledge as an andragogic competency within any prison officer training programme as a result.

DRAMATURGICAL INTERACTION AS A FORM OF LEARNING

Erving Goffman (1963, 1969, 1971) wrote of the 'dramaturgical' interactions which occur between people in particular contexts as a part of his critique of symbolic interactionism. Prison officers develop their own culture of communications when dealing with each other, and this is often reflected in their training and mentoring. In Ireland there is a strong tradition of communicating through storytelling, as social events and cultural mores are passed on over time. This tradition is alive and well in the Irish Prison Service (IPS), where training and mentoring occurs through both official procedures and unofficial processes. This combination of socialised interaction and formal training can be best understood when listing to the stories of the training officers who relayed their experiences over time, locating this 'socialised mentoring' into a context which provides the frame of reference for the recruits to come to better understandings of how they could learn competencies through social exchanges or stories:

> Sharing stories, either personal or second hand, is one way in which these attitudes are transmitted. Through these stories and casual discussions, recruits begin to form an understanding of ... how they are supposed to act.

In the case of the Irish Prison Service, there is a need to recognise the extent of unofficial mentoring which occurs alongside our official training methods. The IPS doesn't include mentors in their ranking system. The role is done voluntarily, but participation is considered when promotions are awarded. I would include two types of mentoring under this heading. The first is the constructive mentoring where best practice is presented by experienced officers, leading to affirmative and positive responses in new recruits. However, this unofficial approach also allows for a second form of mentoring, which I see as negative mentoring. Here, negative and unhelpful socialisation can occur, and recruits may be led into poor professional practices as a result.

In the IPS, training and mentoring is competency-based; skills are demonstrated and behaviour is learned over time in a manner which Waddington (1983) has described as 'a process of copying behaviour' through the mentoring of recruits by experienced staff. However, the levels of experience may vary from institution to institution. In Dublin's Wheatfield Prison, 50% of staff have less than 5 years experiences inside the jail. Across the city in the old Mountjoy Jail, personnel have had a much longer average duration of service. The process of socialised mentoring often begins with a qualified ice-breaker. For example the mentor asks: 'Do you want me to show you how to search a cell without provoking the inmates?' This allows the mentor a way out if the mentee responds in a negative manner to the request-no order was given, so the mentoring process remains relaxed and intact. The suggestion of the mentor is in fact an ice-breaker; the mentee can turn down this suggestion without being seen to be too antagonistic. This allows confidence to develop between mentor and mentee and allows a better interpersonal relationship to develop in a non-judgemental manner. The proviso of 'do you want to know' also protects the experienced officer, who is acting in an unofficial capacity as a mentor.

This unofficial capacity is also reflected in other roles in the IPS; for instance, hostage negotiators like mentors get no financial reward or rank from their efforts, but those who command these roles inevitably go up for promotion. As a result, their experience is often lost to potential mentees, leading to inconsistencies in the unofficial training processes. This may compound the negative mentoring process, as recruits are left exposed to the influence of the negative mentor, who remain in their posts over time. The negative mentor may also try harder to influence the mentee, in order to add to his sphere of influence amongst existing personnel.

This is further reason for a more structured system of mentoring in the IPS, as this would reduce some of the more detrimental aspects of the informal mentoring process. Mentoring in the IPS can therefore be seen to be based on certain processes including pro-social modelling, whereby mentoring is achieved through positive demonstrations of how do things correctly. This is done without evaluation, so as not to prejudice the mentor–mentee relationship. Such approaches are reflective of the 'sounding-board' approach to mentoring taken by the IPS, where mentoring is done in a non-supervisory manner. No formal offer of mentoring is made, rather a demonstration or story is provided to explain and contextualise processes to the recruit. Essentially, the mentor is more like a professional confident, leaving the mentee able to confess to inadequacies and shortcomings in a more relaxed manner. The mentor is however placed in the dilemma of not being able to report issues of concern to the IPS which are revealed as a part of this confidential relationship. Consequentially, guidelines are required for mentoring, even in this unofficial aspect. Mentors in the IPS need to be recognised, particularly as they are not rewarded financially for their work. While mentoring does provide a pathway for promotion, this occurs at the discretion of senior officers who observe unofficial mentoring, which again may be inconsistent.

STORYTELLING AS 'ANECDOTAL MENTORING'

In the traditions of the IPS, anecdotal storytelling has created a mentoring narrative derived from the pool of work-related knowledge held in store by experienced officers. Liebling and Price (2001) have written about the culture of storytelling in the British prison system; this is also the case in Ireland. The British system is also based on unofficial mentoring. In the United States, a culture of developing leadership is more prevalent. In this section of the interview, the Training Officers who are involved in mentoring with the IPS present evidence of how the unofficial forms of mentoring occur in the Irish case. Their comments opened with the following sentiments: 'Things were easier in the past, we could train recruits in a way which was based on learning from mistakes in a controlled environment. We now have to be more careful about everything. There was also a culture where behaviour was monitored but mistakes were punished by making an example of someone'. There were traditional (and humorous) stories of haphazard self-handcuffing incidents which served as cautionary tales and created an emphasis on concentration and focus on the job. This idea of prison folklore and 'poetic justice' was also reflected in the jail humour shared by officers and passed on to recruits as part of a socialised approach to mentoring.

Adopting such a relaxed approach allowed for the development of confidence in what can be a very tense and difficult job; however, humour served two purposes here. It provided a relaxed atmosphere for mentees to learn in, and it provided anecdotal evidence that mistakes could be made and recovered and learned from.

To understand how information selection occurs as part of the development of a recruit's confidence in the advice on offer during the early stage of their posting, we can see how a process of elimination occurs. Recruits would initially ask 10 officer's advice, but over a few weeks this would be reduced to just a few as good providers of accurate advice were located amongst the staff. The culture of prisons meant that all officers would provide an answer whether they were sure of its accuracy, in order that they would be seen to be knowledgeable to the recruits. While this process was inconsistent, it does allow the recruit to combine advice with their own experience over time, and allows for the developing of confidence and competency in a discerning manner. A necessary balance between advice and experience was therefore achieved by the recruit as a result.

FEAR, RESISTANCE AND THE LEARNING PROCESS

Unofficial mentoring also produces a good learning model for teaching recruits that fear in the face of violent situations is a natural and at times necessary part of the job. Many experienced officers relate that they spent so many years pretending not to be afraid until they eventually found that they had lost their initial fears. Prison officers are in a position where they must be convinced of the correctness of their actions in moments of crisis; therefore learning to manage (rather than overcoming) fear is a significant part of the job. It is often a case of learning correct practices from experience, while learning who will provide the best advice in such situations. This is often a matter of serendipity; recruits are at the mercy of the prison's roster detail. Many prisons have a shift that seems to operate better than their colleagues. Again, these processes lead to an inconsistent mentoring experience for the recruit.

Despite sporadic episodes of violence, there is much routine in prisons; the recruit must learn to deal with the two through a process of observation and method. However, even this may cause a misleading form of mentoring to occur, as things come to be done for appearances sake. By adapting a culture of socialised mentoring, organisational assumptions can be made. Experienced personnel may forget what the learning process was like, and this would impact on the experience of the mentee. The dramaturgical processes first identified by Erving Goffman can surface as experienced staff use the internal language of the prison, a language that is lost on the new recruit. Other forms of dynamic security must also be learned from experience, this can be an intimidating process. Moreover, behaviour is often contextualised within the prison's walls. Essentially, behaviour in prison can be understood through the following processes:

- Presentation of the self: 'Dramaturgical' acting in the process of learning
- Learned Behaviour: Learning how to behave from experienced mentors
- Contextualising: Adapting to the different situations presented in prisons
- Perceptions: Extending understanding of these prison contexts.

These processes serve to breakdown some of the resistance, scepticism, fear and inexperience of the recruit, while simultaneously developing their resilience and confidence in their own capacities within the prison. Here, the chief officers take on an important role as managers; the chief can identify potential mentors amongst their officers. While mentoring is voluntary, participation also identifies those who are ambitious to contribute and to move up the career ladder within the service. In general, potential mentors will be identified from their competence and confidence on the job. The mentor must also be resilient as they face their own vulnerability in the early part of the mentoring process; the mentee may choose not to follow their informal advice, posing a personal and professional dilemma for the mentor.

It is here that the socialised stories which provide the subtext for mentoring in the IPS come to most significant; mentors are protected within the informal process of unofficial mentoring. In some ways, the informal nature of mentoring in the IPS allows the mentor to always appear to be 'in control' and provides a degree of calmness for both mentor and mentee. This in turn breeds confidence in the mentoring process, despite its unofficial capacity. As recruits react to incidents within the prison, events can be explained and contextualised – but only when the mentee asks the question of their mentor. The mentor provides the context and confidence for this question by their calm demeanour, despite their own internalised concerns. Here, the relationship is truly dramaturgical.

This professional composure is most apparent when dealing successfully with violent situations. Initially, a composed demeanour is in many ways projected through the officer's uniform and equipment. For many, it becomes a type of armour, shielding the inhabitant from external threats and internal fears. This can be positive or negative, and needs to be managed by the mentor. Mentors often ask recruits about this at the training centre. Questions such as 'How does it feel to wear the uniform' are often met with an array of responses ranging from 'I feel more powerful' to 'we all look the same'. Others can hide behind the uniform. This transformation is another example of the 'dramaturgical performance' of officers in their role in the prisons. From the development of professional confidence and calmness, an appearance of being in control can be developed. Ultimately, the appearance of control also provides a degree of fluidity for the mentor's own dramaturgical performance. The recruit is likely to miss key points or observations during training or actual incident.

Anecdotal mentoring also provides an opportunity for training through de-briefing, as mentees are brought through the episode retrospectively, with an emphasis on developing competencies. This can be a daily occurrence initially while the recruit comes to terms with their new environment. Mentors may have an exclusive mentoring relationship, or it could occur with different personnel at different times. While this informality is conducive to less pressured environments for learning, it may lead to an uneven and contingent experience for the mentee.

From the perspective of the mentor, while the pragmatic aspect of helping to train a recruit's competencies are easily understood as underpinning the mentoring experience, many mentors are not sure of the bounds of their role in the unofficial context. What they are focussed on is the passing on of 'common-sense' approaches to issues which occur within the prison. This practical mentoring is demonstrated when the recruit is brought through the various procedures which occur in the cells, landings and during the transporting of prisoners.

The process is three-fold. First, the mentor demonstrates a procedure to the mentee. Then, the mentee or protégé undertakes the procedure with the support of the mentor. Finally, the mentee begins to work without the mentor (while being observed from a distance). The success of this process is dependent on the pro-social modelling of the mentor, and from the wider team on their roster. This can vary from group to group and from institution to institution. Anecdotal evidence points to many institutions having a 'dark side' and a 'good side' to their rosters, where pro or anti-social modelling may be the prevalent ethos.

The use of 'dynamic security' is another important part of developing the confidence of the mentee within the day-to-day handling of the inmate population. The use of dynamic security measures provides for increased competencies in dealing with issues, but allows the mentee to gain the confidence of his peers and of the inmates, who are also observing the new recruits. The procedures that appear to be out of the hands of the recruit during the initial mentoring process are 'handed over' by the mentor as professional competencies are developed. Again communications and post incident de-briefings are used to underpin experiences gained through dynamic security processes. Nonetheless, some officers are more adept at de-briefing sessions than others, and may be better able to explain incidents in a relaxed manner. Mentoring is often about allowing the recruit to make a contribution.

This can be seen in the development of the recruit's observational capacities. Observation is a major part of the prison officer's job. Good observation includes understanding the contexts and processes of prison, and knowing when to let things go. In many ways, it's about understanding human behaviour. Pro-social teaching encourages the mentee to develop their observational skills through learned processes, rather than every step being explained in detail. Here, mentors also appreciate the value of the mentoring process, as the team begins to benefit from the observations of the recruit. As the mentee is seen to contribute to the roster through their observations, confidence is developed amongst the team, enhancing the mentoring process.

THE INSTITUTIONAL CONTEXT

The institutional context has a large influence on mentoring processes. While the IPS has developed an unofficial approach to mentoring, this needs to be supported by official mentoring procedures. New prisons have a better chance of developing good mentoring culture than old ones. In the Irish older prisons (some built in the middle of the 1800s), old anti-social modelling habits had to be contended with and overcome. In the unusual world of the prison, disturbances provide an opportunity to re-introduce good practices. In many institutions, execution of procedures may become lax over time. The new recruit will replicate what he or she observes in relation to lax practices. A new regime which would be introduced after a disturbance will provide the opportunity to return to a harder line and a clean regime. Prisoners will begin to commit to the new procedures, and come to be dependent on their new routines. This also creates peer-mentoring opportunities for officers to work with prisoners, to help them complete their sentences without breaking rules.

Therefore, the procedural processes of an institution become of paramount importance for the introduction of a positive mentoring atmosphere in a prison. By establishing this improved regime, the context for mentoring is also enhanced. In many ways, mentoring is about developing relationships within the institution. This included peer-mentoring and the mentoring of prisoners. Recruits must learn to understand the dynamic of these relationships as part of the observations. Many recruits get into conflict with prisoners by being over officious in this early stage of their training. They rely on rules, where the experience officer comes to rely on the strength of their relationships with fellow officers and prisoners. The experienced officer would always look to develop a relationship with a prisoner, rather than always reinforcing 'the rules'. Here, the officer is also contributing to a prisoner's rehabilitation, again in an unofficial context.

However, it is here that the narratives of mentoring processes are woven. From this narrative, a culture has evolved, which allows the space for the unofficial mentoring process to develop in a flexible manner. Where the mentee has concerns about their fears or concerns about their own abilities, the mentor can provide an example of how they dealt with their own fears. This admission of vulnerability reinforces the recruit's own self-believe, in addition to instilling a belief that difficult situations can be overcome despite the very human fears experienced in the process. This acknowledgement of personal fear is central to the dramaturgical process of the prison officer's daily working life.

Here the storytelling tradition of the Irish Prison Service is seen in its most beneficial light; by first remembering and then articulating their own fears, the mentor provides a pathway for the mentee to deal with theirs. This reinforces the positive aspect of the mentoring process for both parties, and allows the recruit to develop resilience and confidence in themselves, their colleagues and the processes of prison life. Externally, the recruit must also deal with misinformed public opinion shaped by a tabloid approach to prison stories by the press, as well as learning to leave the pressures of work behind when returning to his family in between shifts.

Inevitably, such cultural connotations have also played a part in the development of the recruit's own perception of what is to be a prison officer before they joined the service. Therefore, the process of developing moral integrity can be seen to be a most difficult one as the recruit is faced with a series of challenges, both external and internal, on the journey to becoming a professional officer who can use their own moral integrity as a basis for performance at work alongside an ongoing process of personal and professional development. Is it possible for the recruit to 'look within' themselves in order to find the capacity necessary to provide the prerequisite professional levels necessary to deal with their own development in congruence with a development in their humane response to those they are dealing with within the prison's walls? In addition, is it possible for the personal integrity of one officer come to shape wider understandings of an institution like a prison?

The answer to this complex moral dilemma can be found in the statements provided in response to these questions by recruits, training officers and governors alike; 'if I can make the difference to just one person than it will all be worthwhile'. Taken in its totality this statement of intent from individuals in the prison service comes to underpin the overall ethos of the Irish Prison Service as a whole by way of their Mission Statement which calls for 'safe, secure and humane custody for people who are sent to prison'. In many ways, the moral integrity of any institution is bound up with the individual integrity of those who serve within it.

Moreover, we can understand the significance of the development of personal levels of moral integrity for the individuals who are to be found on the landings of our prison system dealing with challenging situations such as overcrowding, drug related gang violence and prisoners with intellectual learning disabilities. In such circumstances, each individual situation calls for a decision making process by each officer which depends on a highly developed sense of personal integrity; without this our prisons would be reduced to anarchy. With the abandonment of the development of the extensive prison complex at Thornton Hall in County Dublin, the overcrowding in archaic institutions such as Mountjoy prison continues to be a major challenge to both the competencies and moral integrity of prison officers as well as to that of the nation as a whole.

In that context, how can we come to understand the development of moral integrity amongst our prison officer population? How and why do they continue to maintain a highly developed sense of moral integrity within a system that has left them to deal with many of society's challenging issues such as asylum seekers, multicultural diversity, poverty and marginalisation, drug related gang violence and suicide? What are the virtues of a prison officer who develops their moral integrity in the face of state cut backs and systemic overcrowding? In their chapter 'Prison officers and prison culture' in Yvonne Jewkes' 2007 *Handbook on Prisons*, Alison Liebling and Sara Tait discuss the role of Prison officers, who they see as an under researched group in Penology literature.

The authors criticise the prevailing view of prison officers as being 'power-hungry enforcers of authority', claiming that 'prison work is complex and varied' and that prison officers actually 'under use their authority in the interests of their peacekeeping tasks far more often than they over use it' (Arnold, Liebling, & Tait, 2007, p. 471). They also acknowledge the varied nature of the prison officer's role as it changes from institution to institution. Prison Officers are rarely credited for their work as councillors, as institutional problem solvers, in suicide prevention and in engaging with prisoners by way of rehabilitation.

For instance, any Prison Officers in UK surveys revealed that the camaraderie of their workmates and their role in helping others were significant factors in their motivations for work, despite the fact that many indicated that they had 'fallen into' the job due to financial reasons and had little knowledge of prisons before they signed up (*ibid.*). This data reveals a professional group that has a much more public service-minded attitude than the 'power-hungry' misrepresentations would have many believe. The 'skills' of an effective prison officer include a set of values that require a Prison Officer to be 'loyal to decisions already made', but also 'flexible and able to change opinions when circumstances change', and to have these necessary characteristics:

- Physical characteristics: such as 'verbal skills ... self-confidence, personal authority ... strength for hard working conditions'
- Mental capacity: such as quick thought and retention of various forms of information at once
- Learning ability: such as watching, decision making, problem solving and undertaking administrative tasks
- Interactive ability: such as bearing difficult emotions, understanding other's thoughts and emotions, being interested in one's environment and self, to be sensitive, to have humour, to handle conflict situations ... to be reliable, trustworthy and responsible and to acquire positive energy outside the institution (*ibid.*).

In the Irish case, prison officers are guided by their list of competencies. These competencies include expected items such as 'Situational Awareness' and 'Team Work'. However, there are more pastoral elements within these competencies; items such as 'People Orientation and Caring' and 'Developing Others' demonstrate the positive approach to professional development in the recruit's pathway towards the delivery of custodial care for prisoners and their families who visit them in difficult conditions. This combination of internal and external motivations shape the 'elevation' that Haidt (2003) outlines in his description of the positivity which underpins the professional contribution of those requiring moral capacities in the face of challenging workplace environments. It is only through the combination of internal moral integrity and the reflection of the positive socialisation and mentoring of training officers and fellow professionals that a recruit can set out and maintain the elevation of their endeavour above and beyond the call of duty, while resisting the exhortations or conflicts with those negative mentors who may fall short of such a calling, or the prisoners who are caught up in a sea of personal negativity while in prison.

Once established however, any such negativity can be withstood and overcome by the teaching an evaluation process which Diessner calls 'Systemic Integrity'. This is built on through the extension of personal elevation and moral integrity throughout an institution, with the ultimate creation of systems and institutions that are built on a sense of shared integrity (Diessner, 2007). In many ways, the creation of systemic integrity is similar to a faith-based approach to life; one believer can come to influence the many to observe the codes and rituals of faith. In order for an institution such as a prison to work, there must be many believers, those who subsume their personal concerns for the good of their colleagues, and also for the prisoners in their care. In many ways this mobilisation of elevated or systemic forms of integrity defines the manner in which prisoners experience the primary forms of rehabilitation that occur during the duration of their sentence.

It is the officer with integrity that protects the incarcerated debt-defaulter from the worst aspects of the hardened criminals they may be surrounded by. The Irish justice system imprisons both minor and serious offenders within the walls of its medium security prisons, only paramilitary prisoners and white collar criminals are afforded separate institutions for their periods of incarceration. Therefore, the prison officer must invest a good deal of time in protecting their prisoners; from the gang-related violence they might inflict on each other, from an individual's suicidal tendencies and from the frustration or grief of news delivered by visitors from home. Prison officers also develop their colleagues through mentoring.

From the perspective of prison officers and mentoring, while the pragmatic aspect of helping to train a recruit's competencies are easily understood as underpinning the mentoring experience, many mentors are not sure of the bounds of their role in the unofficial context. What they are focussed on is the passing on of 'common-sense' approaches to issues which occur within the prison. This practical mentoring is demonstrated when the recruit is brought through the various procedures which occur in the cells, landings and during the transporting of prisoners. The process is three-fold. First, the mentor demonstrates a procedure to the mentee. Then, the mentee or protégé undertakes the procedure with the support of the mentor. Finally, the mentee begins to work without the mentor (while being observed from a distance). The success of this process is dependent on the pro-social modelling of the mentor, and from the wider team on their roster. This can vary from group to group and from institution to institution. Anecdotal evidence points to many institutions having a 'dark side' and a 'good side' to their rosters, where pro or anti-social modelling may be the prevalent ethos (Leonard et al., 2009).

The use of dynamic security is another important part of developing the confidence of the mentee within the day-to-day handling of the inmate population. The use of dynamic security measures provides for increased competencies in dealing with issues, but allows the mentee to gain the confidence of his peers and of the inmates, who are also observing the new recruits. The procedures that appear to be out of the hands of the recruit during the initial mentoring process are 'handed over' by the mentor as professional competencies are developed. Again communications and post incident de-briefings are used to underpin experiences gained through dynamic security processes.

Nonetheless, some officers are more adept at de-briefing sessions than others, and may be better able to explain incidents in a relaxed manner. Mentoring is often about allowing the recruit to make a contribution. This can be seen in the development of the recruit's observational capacities. Observation is a major part of the prison officer's job. Good observation includes understanding the contexts and processes of prison, and knowing when to let things go. In many ways, it's about understanding human behaviour. Pro-social teaching encourages the mentee to develop their observational skills through learned processes, rather than every step being explained in detail. Here, mentors also appreciate the value of the mentoring process, as the team begins to benefit from the observations of the recruit. As the mentee is seen to contribute to the roster through their observations, confidence is developed amongst the team, enhancing the 'elevated' mentoring process (*ibid.*).

TEACHING THE 'SOCIOLOGICAL IMAGINATION' TO PRISON OFFICERS

The shift in ideological emphasis away from left and liberal concerns with the disadvantaged background of offenders in the 1970s and 1980s has given way to a right-realist emphasis on the victim, and on punitive regimes that extract some form of retribution on those seen to trespass laws and social contexts. For many, these contexts are far too often bound up with the social background of the offender, leading to an over representation of certain social groups within prisons, as power relations between dominant and marginalised sectors of society come to be reflected in successive arrest and incarceration statistics.

This point is illustrated when recruits were taught about Anthony Gidden's (2006) adaptation of C. Wright Mill's 'sociological imagination' which he relates through an account of the extensive social processes surrounding a cup of coffee. We can apply this understanding of the wider sociological understanding to other everyday objects which take on entirely different meanings in a different social setting. For instance, if we think of everyday objects such as a key, a pack of cigarettes, a belt, a gate, a kitchen knife or a toothbrush, they carry certain accepted social understandings in a domestic context.

SHAPING UNDERSTANDINGS OF DEVIANCE

The globalisation of criminal activity has provided a backdrop towards the growth of what Christie termed 'the crime control industry'. States which were used to dealing with identifiable local threats from indigenous crime gangs have had to adapt to the onset of a multinational crime sector, where those orchestrating crimes have access to global networks of cohorts, materials and customers. Some of the more audacious criminal figures have been known to make contact with the media through mobiles, as the cult of personality has come to include crime figures who attempt to embody the lifestyle depicted in television programmes such as *Love/Hate*, *the Wire* or *the Sopranos* or movies such as *Natural Born Killers*, *the Godfather* series or Al Pacino's role as a violent drug dealer in *Scarface*. The recruits were also given an outline of how Durkheim outlined the significance of tradition and commemoration through time as an important element in the creation of moral and legal codes for a developing society. For Durkheim, there is a relationship between the marking of important dates or milestones and the establishment of norms.

The recruits were then taught about the 'Zimbardo's Prison Experiment', which provided the extreme behavioural outcomes described in his 2007 book *The Lucifer Effect: Understanding How Good People Turn Evil*. In Zimbardo's 1971 experiment, students adopted roles of either guards or prisoners. Within a short period of time, those volunteering as guards began to abuse the 'prisoners' in their care, causing stress and anxiety in those volunteering as prisoners. Zimbardo cut short his experiment due to the extreme reaction of the 'guards'. While it is clear the experiment was not congruent with the environment of a real prison, the Zimbardo experiment demonstrates the problem caused when those in authority behave in a deviant manner to those in their care. These findings were then contrasted with a discussion about the abuses caused by the US military in Guantanamo Bay and Abu Ghraib during the Gulf War.

SOCIOLOGICAL UNDERSTANDINGS OF PRISON CULTURE

In their chapter 'Prison officers and prison culture' from Yvonne Jewkes' 2007 *Handbook on Prisons* Helen Arnold, Alison Liebling and Sara Tait discuss the role of Prison officers, who they see as an under researched group in Sociological and Criminology or Penology based literature. They criticise the prevailing view of prison officers as being 'power-hungry enforcers of authority', claiming that 'prison work is complex and varied' and that prison officers actually 'under use their authority in the interests of their peacekeeping tasks far more often than they over use it' (Arnold et al., 2007, p. 471). They also acknowledge the varied nature of the prison officer's role as it changes from institution to institution.

The culture of prison as an aspect of society is one which is barely understood, and often distorted by tabloid media stories. The recruits pointed out that they are rarely credited for their work as councillors, as institutional problem solvers, in suicide prevention and in engaging with prisoners by way of rehabilitation. Many prison officers in UK surveys revealed that the camaraderie of their workmates and their role in helping others were significant factors in their motivations for work, despite the fact that many indicated that they had 'fallen into' the job due to financial reasons and had little knowledge of prisons before they signed up (*ibid.*). This data reveals a professional group that has a much more public service-minded attitude than the 'power-hungry' misrepresentations would have many believe.

The 'skills' of an effective prison officer include a set of values that require a prison officer to be 'loyal to decisions already made', but also 'flexible and able to change opinions when circumstances change'. The ethical and moral performance of UK prisons was the subject of a further study by Liebling (2004). Here, differences in the 'Values and Emotional Climates' of the various prisons was outlined, despite the 'similarity of function' charged to each institution.

CONCLUDING REMARKS

The full extent of supports that a prison officer provides to the prisoner is not fully understood or appreciated within our society. The concept of integrity posited by Diessner provides us with the conceptual framework for understanding the internal process undertaken by prison officers in the course of delivering a service of custodial care to those unfortunate enough to find themselves incarcerated with the prison system. The professional competencies and humane ethos of the Irish Prison Service's mission statement provides us with the context for the elevation through service which is the bedrock of the prison officer's service to the prisoner in their care. Ultimately, it is this combination of teaching personal integrity and professional elevation which provided the recruits with the answer to some of the dilemmas they faced behind the prison walls, and thereby provide an indication to wider society the nature of service provided by the custodians of our prisons in the face of ongoing challenges such as overcrowding, economic constraints and violence from the prison population. Achieving elevated integrity and competency at work also begins the important process of primary rehabilitation for prisoners, who are more likely to respond in a positive manner to this form of interaction.

The extent to which the officer delivers on this elevated form of professional integrity is not always recognised, sometimes even by the officers themselves who see themselves as 'just doing their job'. Teaching them about social issues and pro-social competencies enhanced their ability to attain levels of professional integrity also inspires their colleagues to achieve the same. However, like their colleagues in the Gardai, nursing sector, social work, social care, fire service and ambulances, prison officers deliver a form of professional care which requires a commitment to service to others. The extent to which the programme succeeded in their attempts to maintain an elevated degree of integrity and competency within their professional careers can be understood within a wider context of an evolving re-assessment of the issues of crime and punishment which affects all within Irish society.

REFERENCES

Arnold, H., Liebling, A., & Tait, S. (2007). Prison officers and prison culture. In Y. Jewkes (Ed.), *Handbook on prisons* (pp. 471–495). Cullompton, Devon: Willan Publishing.

Bennet, J., Crewe, B., & Wahidin, A. (2007). *Understanding prison staff*. London: Willian.

Cherry, S. (2004). *Transforming behaviour*. London: Willian.

Coyle, A. (2005). *Understanding prisons: Key issues in policy and practice*. London: Open University Press.

Crawley, E. (2004). *Doing prison work: The public and private lives of prison officers*. London: Willan.

Diessner, R. (2007). Integrity: Psychological, moral, and spiritual. *Human Development Journal, 28*(3), 5–10.

Edgar, K., O'Donnell, I., & Martin, C. (2004). *Prison violence: The dynamics of conflict, fear and power*. London: Willan.

Giddens, A. (2006). *Introduction to sociology* (Vol. 5). Cambridge: Polity.

Goffman, A. (1969). *Strategic interaction*. Philadelphia, PA: University of Pennsylvania Press.

Goffman, E. (1971). *Relations in public: Micro studies of the public order*. London: Basic Books.

Haidt, J. (2003). Elevation and the positive psychology of morality. In C. L. M. Keyes & J. Haidt (Eds.), *Flourishing: Positive psychology and the life well-lived* (pp. 275–289). Washington, DC: American Psychological Association.

Howe, J. (2012). *An examination of reflective writings of recruit prison officers, to evaluate the achievement of learning outcomes*. Unpublished MA thesis. University of Limerick.

Jewkes, Y. (2007). *Handbook on prisons*. London: Wilian, Helen Arnold.

Leonard, L., Kenny, P., & McGuckin, J. (2009). The mentoring processes of the Irish prison service: A sociological inquiry. *American Jails*, April–May 2009.

Liebling, A. (2011). Moral performance, in human and degrading treatment, and prison pain. *Punishment and Society*, *13*(5), 530–550.

Liebling, A. assisted by H. Arnold (2004). *Prisons and their moral performance: A study of values, quality and prison life*. Oxford: Oxford University Press.

Liebling, A., & Price, D. (2001). *The prison officer*. Leyhill: HM Prison Service.

Liebling, A., Price, D., & Shefer, G. (2011). *The prison officer* (2nd ed.). Cullompton, Devon: Willan Publishing.

Rogers, C. R. (1961). *On becoming a person*. New York, NY: Harper & Row.

Waddington, P. A. (1983). *The training of prison governors*. London: Croom Helm Ltd.

Zimbardo, P. (2007). *The Lucifer Effect: Understanding how good people turn evil*. London: Random House.

INDEX

Printed and bound by CPI Group (UK) Ltd, Croydon, CR0 4YY

13/09/2026

14961058-0008